Self-Discipline

How to Build Mental Toughness and Develop a Success Mindset to Achieve Your Life's Goals

Robert Craig

© Copyright 2020 by Robert Craig - All rights reserved.

This document is geared towards providing exact and reliable information in regards to the topic and issue covered. The publication is sold with the idea that the publisher is not required to render accounting, officially permitted, or otherwise, qualified services. If advice is necessary, legal or professional, a practiced individual in the profession should be ordered.

- From a Declaration of Principles which was accepted and approved equally by a Committee of the American Bar Association and a Committee of Publishers and Associations.

In no way is it legal to reproduce, duplicate, or transmit any part of this document in either electronic means or in printed format. Recording of this publication is strictly prohibited and any storage of this document is not allowed unless with written permission from the publisher. All rights reserved.

The information provided herein is stated to be truthful and consistent, in that any liability, in terms of inattention or otherwise, by any usage or abuse of any policies, processes, or directions contained within is the solitary and utter responsibility of the recipient reader. Under no circumstances will any legal responsibility or blame be held against the publisher for any reparation, damages, or monetary loss due to the information herein, either directly or indirectly.

Respective authors own all copyrights not held by the publisher.

The information herein is offered for informational purposes solely, and is universal as so. The presentation of the information is without contract or any type of guarantee assurance.

The trademarks that are used are without any consent, and the publication of the trademark is without permission or backing by the trademark owner. All trademarks and brands within this book are for clarifying purposes only and are the owned by the owners themselves, not affiliated with this document.

Table of Content

INTRODUCTION: 1

CHAPTER 1 INTRODUCTION TO SELF-DISCIPLINE 3

1.1 Defining Self-Discipline 3

1.2 Manifestation of Self-Discipline 5

1.3 Importance of Self-Discipline 7

1.4 Self-Discipline as a Skill 10

1.5 Benefits of Self-Discipline 15

CHAPTER 2 DEVELOPING SELF-DISCIPLINE 18

2.1 Elements of Self-Discipline 18

2.2 Techniques for Strengthen Self-Discipline 23

2.3 Pillars of Self-Discipline 28

2.4 Developing Daily Habits for Programming Mind 30

2.5 Self-Discipline Exercises 37

CHAPTER 3 IMPORTANCE OF SELF-DISCIPLINE IN CHILDHOOD 40

3.1 Childhood Emotional Neglect 40

3.2 Importance of Teaching Self-Discipline 44

3.3 Ways to Teach Self-Discipline to Kids 46

3.4 Steps to Build Self-Discipline and Willpower in Students 51

3.5 Secret of Raising a Self-Disciplined Child 54

3.6 Self-Discipline Leads To School Success 58

CHAPTER 4 SELF-DISCIPLINE AND PERSONALITY 61

4.1 Becoming a Disciplined Person 62

4.2 Qualities of Self-Disciplined Person 65

4.3 Characteristic of Self-Discipline Achievers 67

4.4 Creating Internal Strength 70

4.5 Factors That Affect Self-Discipline 72

4.6 Lack of Self-Discipline 74

4.7 How to Become Self-Disciplined 77

CHAPTER 5 SELF-DISCIPLINE IN LIFE 79

5.1 Discipline Begins At Home 79

5.2 Method for Gaining Self-Discipline in Everyday Life 81

5.3 Self-Discipline: Key to Health and Wealth 86

5.4 Self-Discipline at Workplace 93

CHAPTER 6 MASTERING SELF-DISCIPLINE 100

6.1 Ways to Mastering Self-Discipline 100

6.2 Building Mental Toughness 104

6.3 Improving Will Power for Better Self-Discipline 107

6.4 The Strength and Stamina of Willpower 109

6.5 Self-Discipline Is a Key to Success 113

6.6 Secrets of Self-Discipline 118

7. CONCLUSION 124

8. REFERENCES: 126

Introduction:

Self-discipline is an art of maintaining better control over one's own life, the decisions one makes, and the choices one makes in one's life. Self-discipline is characterized by an individual who works perfectly on goals or agendas already set for achieving success.

A self-disciplined person can do it properly at the right time, to prepare, and to behave according to the goals set. Self-discipline can, therefore, be defined by having a person's ability by which he or she acts according to his or her conscience, knowledge, and experience to achieve the maximum goals and objectives.

Discipline has considerable value in human lives. There are two types of Discipline, which are the reason behind the success of many individuals in this world. The discipline part more closely related to one's nature. It is externally experienced.

The other type of Discipline, in contrast, is more related to one's behavior. Externally, it is learnt. With one's contact with other like-minded fellows, this sort of Discipline is taught. Nonetheless, all forms of Discipline are highly crucial in today's life.

Discipline is essential in every corner of our lives. We can't have success and desired results in our classrooms, colleges, universities, offices, or even at battlefields without applying Discipline to our lives. In many ways, Discipline helps us.

Firstly, preparation helps us make our objectives realistic. It helps us distinguish and prioritize critical daily tasks.

With the aid of training, we learn to make better use of time.

A disciplined man knows how to prioritize his goals to achieve the desired goals and create an active policy.

A self-disciplined man knows precisely where he stands. He is capable of successfully figuring out every issue. With self-discipline, proper planning, and timely planning execution, we can be successful when faced with any obstacle.

In this universe, Discipline is the core of everything. We observe that in this universe, everything works appropriately as per planning. The sunrise and sunset, the seasonal exchange, the fall of nights and days, life and death, etc... All work on a perfect discipline. There are many manifestations of Discipline in our culture; that is, there are.

Therefore we can never deny the meaning, worth, and significance of Discipline in our lives. For boys, girls, students, and people from all walks of life, it's essential. In our lives, we should be taking the habit of self-discipline. Only this way will we make our lives productive.

Chapter 1 Introduction to Self-Discipline

Discipline is the method of training the mind, body, or behaviour, and it makes people do what is expected of them. People often confuse "Discipline "with "Physical punishment, "but they are quite different. Discipline is about teaching. It is not necessary to physically punish to teach an individual what they need to know. The purpose of discipline is to guide a person to choose what is right through teaching and learning rather than forces.

Self-Discipline is about your ability to control your desires and impulses for long enough to stay focused on what needs to get done to achieve your goal successfully. It's about taking small, consistent daily action that helps yours from critical habits that support your objectives. Self-Disciple is how your self-control is gained and the way our hope is maintained. The vigour of our concerns is affected by the warmth of our desires.

1.1 Defining Self-Discipline

Discipline comes from the Latin word "Disciplinary," which means to teach, instruct, and educate.

Discipline is defined as training or melding of the mind and character to bring about desired behaviours. It is merely a "Good Behaviour." A situation where there are no issues, disorders, chaos, confusion, disobedience, misconduct, etc.

Whereas Self-Discipline means that you have to be very determined to achieve the goals you have set. It is the ability to get yourself to take action regardless of your emotional state.

According to the dictionary," Self-Discipline is the ability to control yourself and to make yourself work hard or behave in a particular way without needing anyone else to tell you what to do.

Self-Discipline can also be defined as "Correction or regulation of oneself for the sake of improvement."

In medical terms, Self-Discipline is defined as" training and control of oneself and one's conduct, usually for personal improvement."

- Occurs in different forms, such as perseverance, patience, resilience, thought before doing, completing what you begin to do, and as the ability to execute your own decisions and strategies, given difficulty, challenges, or obstacles.

- Often means self-control, the desire to prevent excessive excesses of anything that could have negative impacts.

- Of the main features of self-discipline is the ability to discontinue instantaneous and immediate gratification and pleasure in favor of some more significant gain or more satisfying outcomes, even if this requires effort and time?

- Word self-discipline often creates some anxiety and resistance due to the mistaken notion that it is uncomfortable, difficult to achieve, and requires a great deal of effort and sacrifice. In reality, exercising and practicing self-discipline can be enjoyable, requires no strenuous effort, and the benefits are fantastic.

- Self-discipline is not, as some people think, a punishing or restrictive lifestyle, and it has nothing to do with narrow-mindedness. It is the source of inner strength and staying power, crucial to coping with the daily affairs and achieving goals.

- With willpower, self-discipline can help you overcome laziness, procrastination, and indecisiveness. These skills allow for action and perseverance with it, even if the work is unpleasant and requires effort.

- Encourages you to practice patience, to become more compassionate, sensitive, respectful, and considerate in what you do. It also helps you endure strain and interference from outside.
- The self-disciplined person is more punctual, investing in what he or she does more time and effort.
- The self-disciplined person has a better chance of taking charge of his or her life, setting goals, and taking practical steps to achieve them.

"Discipline just means our ability to get things done when we don't want to."

Self-Discipline According to Psychology

Self-discipline is a learned character trait--no one is born with it. It impacts every area of your life and is your ability to pursue your goals and do what is right, regardless of your weaknesses or how you feel. Self-discipline is established in your body and your mind. Healthy habits create self-discipline.

1.2 Manifestation of Self-Discipline

You can define self-discipline as the exterior manifestation of your inner strength. It is the method of creating a mentality in which you are guided and influenced by your own deliberate choices rather than by other people's bad habits, emotions, circumstances, or sway. It inculcates inside of you the ability to focus your mind and energies on your goals and helps you develop a sense of perseverance and continuity.

The Most Important Ingredient of Success

Self-discipline gives you the ability to stand by your decisions without changing your mind. It gives you the strength to make resolutions, take action, and execute your game plan irrespective of any difficulties, discomfort, or obstacles you may encounter. Self-discipline is, therefore, necessary if you want to live your life on your terms and achieve the goals and objectives you are aiming for.

Learning and developing self-control skills will help you improve other areas of your life, such as:

- Overcome procrastination
- Wake up early in the morning
- Fulfill your promises to yourself and others
- Avoid behaving rashly and on impulse
- Resisting temptations of eating non-healthy foods
- Continue working on your diet to achieve your desired fitness goals
- Continue to work on the project even after the initial excitement has decreased
- Remove temptations whenever necessary
- Recover and learn from mistakes effectively

1.3 Importance of Self-Discipline

The definition of self-discipline is the "correction or self-regulation for the sake of change." This definition means that it is necessary to restrict or discourage ourselves from specific actions if we are going to improve in some way. If we relate this to studying, it means we have to stop doing certain things or start doing certain things while considering to get the positive results that we want. It is incredibly essential to control ourselves in this way because it can create self-esteem. When we attain the goals we set for ourselves, we get a boost of trust that can improve many aspects of our lives.

Self-discipline is one of the best and most important characteristics that everyone should have. This ability is necessary for every area of life, and although most people recognize its value, very few do anything to improve it.

Self-discipline, contrary to common opinion, does not mean being hard on yourself or leading a restrictive, restricted lifestyle. Self-discipline means self-control, which is a sign of your inner strength and self-control, actions, and reactions.

Self-discipline gives you the ability to stick to and obey your decisions, without changing your mind, and is, therefore, one of the essential criteria to achieve goals.

Possession of this ability helps you to persevere with your choices and plans until you get them done. It also acts as an inner strength that allows you to conquer addictions, procrastination, and laziness, and to move on with whatever you do.

One of its main features is the ability to reject instant gratification and enjoyment in favour of some greater reward, which takes time and effort to get it.

Self-discipline is one of the key ingredients for performance. It communicates itself in many different ways:

- Perseverance.
- Despite disappointment and defeats, the desire to not give up.
- Self-control.
- The ability to tolerate threats or temptations.
- Try again and again until you do what you are trying to do.

Life puts obstacles and difficulties on the path to success and accomplishment, and you have to behave with perseverance and determination to rise above them, and this, of course, requires self-discipline.

Possession of this capacity leads to self-confidence and self-esteem, and ultimately to happiness and contentment.

In contrast, lack of self-discipline leads to problems of failure, loss, health and relationships, obesity, and other issues.

Particularly useful is this ability to tackle eating disorders, addictions, smoking, drinking, and bad habits. You will need it to encourage yourself to sit and read, exercise your body, develop new skills, and spiritual growth and meditation for self-improvement.

Benefits from self-discipline and value Self-discipline helps:

- Do not behave rashly or on impulses.
- Complete your obligations to yourself and others.
- Surmounting laziness and procrastination.
- Continue to work on a project, even after the initial rush of enthusiasm has faded away.
- Go to the gym, go walking or swimming, also if your mind tells you to stay home and watch television.

- Continue to work on your diet and overcome the temptation to eat fattening food.

It will be easier for you to strengthen your self-discipline if you:

- Understand its importance in your life.
- Become aware of your undisciplined behaviour and its consequences. When this awareness increases, you will be more convinced of the need to make a change in your life.
- Make an effort to act and behave according to the decisions you make, regardless of laziness, the tendency to procrastinate, or the desire to give up and stop what you are doing.
- You can strengthen your self-disciple, even if it is currently weak, with the help of special simple **exercises**, which you can practice at any time or place.

1.4 Self-Discipline as a Skill

Nobody is born with ingrained self-discipline. If that were the case, then babies and toddlers would adhere to their parents' wishes and sit up straight, not make a mess, and understand every word and thought that their mothers and fathers had. There would also be no requirement for institutions like the military, schools, or juvenile detention or prisons, as the common ills of society would be eliminated simply by appealing to the public's genetic predisposition to exercise discipline in their daily lives. Alas, as we all well know, this world does not exist.

Self-discipline is a rare commodity. Why? Because it's hard; people are shying away from the hard and painful stuff. And rightly so.

We were biologically programmed to avoid conditions that could potentially endanger, kill, or stress us to the point that our bodies have to make more effort than is typically needed to function optimally, or even survive.

This is why most people find discipline so tough.

We're just not geared to disciplining ourselves.

It is, therefore, an ability learned in the same way as any other quality you gain through learning, practice, repetition, and ultimately automation.

"Okay," you ask yourself, "I know it's a talent, but why should I bother with all this stuff of self-discipline?" This is why:

Increased Focus

Everyone has dreams of being better than they are now.

Everyone in heaven wants the brass ring.

Yet very few people have ever achieved this incredible height.

Why? For what?

Because they lack the emphasis people have on discipline.

We get distracted by the things that are going to give them instant gratification and make them feel better.

Discipline people have strong expectations behind them, with good why.

They've developed the habit of remaining on the job to get where they need to be.

More than likely, they achieved this by looking into the future and seeing themselves in an alternative reality where they didn't do the research and thus ended up in even worse condition than they are now.

Instead, they ignored the distractions, focused on what they wanted, created systems that made them move in the right direction and achieved what they set out to do precisely.

Increased Activity

Disciplined people are active individuals.

We prioritize action over inaction and take the necessary steps to get the job done, even if they don't feel like it.

Yet they aren't robots.

They can relax after the work is done or celebrate their successes, but they don't rest on their laurels.

Because of the systems and habits, they have implemented in their daily routine, and the disciplined person prioritizes physical fitness, healthy eating, sleep, personal hobbies, work, and family time in ways that allow them to accomplish all these things and still have time left over for any other activities.

As a result of all this increased activity, they have more stability than the average person who seeks to vegetate when they do not.

Healthier Lifestyle

Discipline is at the core of any healthy lifestyle.

Without it, you could not possibly have robust physical health.

In any sports, think of all the elite athletes.

How have they reached the level that so few of us will ever experience in our lifetimes?

We worked harder than anyone else and were able to do more consistently than the average person.

Those are fields.

However, they did

Better Self-Control

The main reason so many of us aren't where we want to be in our financial life, our relationships, health, and spiritual well-being is that we can't control our urges and vices.

We think Thug life but end up going mental because we're punishing ourselves unnecessarily, doing what others do just because that's the' done thing' without realizing the damage it's doing to our souls.

A conscientious person has more self-control over themselves and their acts.

They do things that benefit them and move them toward their dreams, whatever happens around them.

Their preferences in diet, physical activity, socializing, how they spend their free time, and the partners they choose are conscientious.

By being disciplined, people who are unaware of their actions and words have and tend to lead much more comfortable and rewarding lives to avoid regular conflicts and problems.

More time

You will find that, when you are more disciplined, you have more time to do other things you want to do.

By having regular systems in place and practicing healthy, positive habits daily and adhering to a disciplined routine, the day tends to open up for you and finding the time to be with family, friends, and colleagues suddenly become much less of an issue than it will be for disciples

More respect

Respect orders discipline

The disciplined life is a rough and exhausting life that very few among us will ever really know.

Therefore, the people who walk among us who have exceptional levels of concentration, motivation, action, energy, and achievement are idolized, envied, and looked up by others who don't have the same capacities.

This has several reasons:

- Being a disciplined person is difficult, and those who want that same intensity level will respect you.
- You gain the respect of your fellow employees and bosses if you are an employee who finishes their job regularly on time and at a high standard.
- Being consistent with your studies lets you complete your test training, tasks, and homework promptly, which improves your chances of getting top marks.

- Speaking about research.

Better Academic Performance

Discipline helps in two ways for your academic performance.

Firstly, when teachers are disciplined, there is a structure in their classes, a wealth of knowledge, and a happier student body. The students pay more attention to their teachers when the curriculum is run with an emphasis on discipline, and the syllabus is taught in its entirety and promptly.

Second, students who are diligent in their studies are doing well in the classroom as well as in exams and assignments. Disciplined lives in the home allow them sufficient time for research, rest, and play.

The combination of these produces a stable, lively atmosphere in which students can excel and become valuable social contributors.

A Happier Life

- Equals freedom.
- You are a disciplined person, every aspect of your life improves, and you experience increased physical, emotional, financial, and spiritual growth and success by practicing discipline in every dimension.
- Life of restraint is no perfect life.
- Will never get in the way in an ideal world.
- In the real world, we all have to deal with our obligations, challenges, vices, and weaknesses.
- The best way to handle all of them is by discipline.
- Focusing on doing what needs to be done consistently and remaining calm when the challenges of life arise, you will have better health, wealth, relationships, and, ultimately, a better experience.

1.5 Benefits of Self-Discipline

Once you set out on the path to self-discipline (Your life will be changing significantly), and through patience and perseverance, there are countless benefits.

Your values are clear goals lined up, interests aligned and stable self-discipline, all go hand in hand. If you know the result that you're after and have fully established your muscle self-discipline, then you have no trouble putting things first. Distractions have no power over your life anymore. This increases concentration.

- Decision making transforms into a breeze. It cuts down on uncertainties and confusion.
- Life becomes structured
- The way you look at life changes.

You are at Your Control Isn't that incredible sound?!!! Being your life's Boss? Mastering yourself, and getting your priorities straight? Setting targets and reaching them? Procrastination can no longer get the best out of you.

That also means;

- Dreams and principles guide you, not impulses and moods influence you.
- Good habits can be adopted, and bad ones can be dug as you please. (And let's not ignore all the advantages that good habits can bring)
- You're less vulnerable to addictions because you're keeping your mind in your pocket instead of giving it to outside powers.
- Your Guilt Goes Down The guilt of failing to do the right thing at the right time has the power to weigh a person

down significantly. Many burdens just make us realize the weight they were born when they are lifted.

When you know your meaning and what you stand for and have power over yourself, you stick to it. The long-term drive for bonuses doesn't let you settle for anything less. This makes you invincible. For now, instant gratification is a pointless trend.

Being true to yourself makes you a happy person who knows the true meaning of fulfilment.

You own a Big Roadblock to Success I You've gone out of your way and got what you want.

You become more self-reliant. The more you can control yourself, the more independent you become. You are more aware of your true potential.

The strengthening of your relationships is a measure of your relationship with others. You cannot keep promises to others when you are unable to keep promises to yourself. You are trustworthy with good self-control.

You save time consistency helps you to do things on time, which will save you a great deal of trouble. There is virtually no last-minute panic and hassle. You become a calmer person, tackling and finishing all your tasks and projects at the right time.

You have room to relax. Now that the most important things are all taken care of, you have free time on your hands. You can have fun at having fun.

Self-discipline also helps to:
- Know your weaknesses
- Wake up early in the morning
- Maintain simple morning routines to transform your life

- Motivation to follow daily routine even if your mind tells you to stay at home
- Mindset motivation
- Remove temptations and negative thoughts
- The power to stick to your decisions and follow them through, without changing your mind
- Reset your mind and stop procrastinating
- Enables you to persevere with your conclusions and plans until you accomplish them
- Set clear goals and have an execution plan
- Continue your work even when tired or enthusiasm has faded away
- Help to overcome addictions, procrastination, and laziness
- Avoid acting rashly
- Self-forgiveness and forgive others
- Fulfill promises you make
- Create new, unusual habits by keeping it simple

Chapter 2 Developing Self-Discipline

One of the essential skills to develop in life is the skill of self-discipline. It is the most critical skill which has to be developed in childhood. If self-discipline skill is not produced in a person, then it will cause you many problems. Such as health problems, distraction, procrastination, financial problems, clutter, things are Piling up and getting overwhelmed, and much more. Developing so is such an important skill, but most people don't know where to begin.

2.1 Elements of Self-Discipline

Self-discipline is the desire to do what you think you ought to be doing something that is focused on your thinking.

You might have an exam tomorrow morning, for example, and your mind tells you that you have to prepare and revise, but you feel bloated, tired, and you want to collapse in front of the TV.

The phenomenon of delayed gratification is closely related to self-discipline. By now delaying the' feel good' factor, you can experience an even greater' feel great' factor at a later stage.

For example, if you decided to study the night before your test instead of collapsing in front of the screen, you might have been more comfortable in your examination, less nervous, and feel more relaxed and calm.

You may have encountered a better result or higher grades as a result, too. In the end, this adds to even more satisfaction.

Understand Yourself

First, to develop self-discipline, you need to consider which areas of your life you are not disciplined in? Where do you wish to become more disciplined? What are the places you are most up against?

What are the three things in your life that you continue to put off, but you know they would make a significant impact if you were to do these?

Write them down and jot down why you don't do them at all. Write down, next to each, why you want to do everyone.

Focus on the Longer Term

What are your expectations in the longer term?

How, in your life, are you trying to accomplish? Focusing on your long-term goals makes you understand why you now have to do something extraordinary. If you had to take action now, what would be the long-term gain you'll get later on?

You may find it very difficult to get over to the gym, for example, or go for a run. If you have to go and do this now, what is the gain you'll get in the longer term? Your health, fitness, and actual wellbeing are all dependent on the action you are taking at this moment.

Schedule Your Time

Scheduling your time is an excellent tool for setting up self-discipline. If you find it impossible to get started writing your book, plan the next seven days for 30 minutes each day and adhere to the time you've committed to it. Before you know it, you'd have spent three and a half hours writing your novel at the end of the week.

Get Started

One of the easiest ways to build self-discipline is simply to get going. The toughest part of doing something you don't want to do is often the fact you don't have a drive. It could sound like a daunting challenge. Run on' just do it' motto. Take the first step, just' press' yourself into taking action.

Reward Yourself

If you do anything now, you're going to get a profit in the future, especially if it helps you achieve your long-term goals. You can, however, bring this to a different level. You don't have to wait to be rewarded until almost the end, and begin to feel good. Award yourself at milestones throughout your project or take. Perhaps, you haven't started a project yet. Tell yourself that if you work on your project for an hour, you'll be rewarded with anything you want to be rewarded with. Give yourself little incentives to help you create your self-discipline throughout the project.

Get Support from Others

Assistance from others can be significant. If you're surrounded by positive people who can inspire you and support your goals, then you're more likely to be successful in what you're tryingtodo.

2.2 Types of Self-Discipline

Self-discipline is an ability to do hard or unpleasant things without someone pushing you or offering you incentives. The basic types of self-discipline are below.

Self-Control

The ability to control your actions and focus your thoughts toward an objective. This includes the ability to block or redirect unproductive or negative emotions. For example, the ability to keep driving well when you are getting angry with other drivers.

Introspection

Introspection is the ability to analyse your feelings, emotions, and character in constructive ways to change them. For starters, the ability to recognize flaws in your thought, such as motivated reasoning.

Self-Direction

In an area of confusion, the ability to produce sensible decisions rapidly. This implies that, if this is required, you can make decisions and behave without input from others. For example, a new hire that thrives without any direction from its boss and team in a dynamic and fast-moving organization.

Focus & Endurance

The ability to concentrate on work, study, listening, and anything else that requires attention over time and keep that focus. For instance, a student who can read a book cover-to-cover effectively doesn't find it especially interesting to finalize a book report.

Habit & Routine

Habit & routine are self-disciplining tools by which a person keeps repeating productive behaviour. For instance, a person who needs to build a healthy body mass having a habit of jogging every morning.

Will Power

Despite a massive motivation to pursue the exercise, the willingness to resolve destructive behaviour and behaviours.

Principled Behaviour

The ability to comply with a set of principles and values. Overall, it's easy to think about the benefits you admire but hard to live up to beliefs in a uniform manner. You may believe, for example, in the golden rule of treating humans as you would wish to be treated, but it's easy to lose self-control with those around you or refuse to see their viewpoint. The matching of your behaviour with your beliefs is a great means of expression, which requires a lot of self-discipline to master.

Personal Resilience

Personal resilience is the ability to keep your discipline in the face of considerable stress. The ability to handle heavy criticism, for example, that creates strong emotions without acting negatively.

Stoicism

Stoicism is an optimum that states that your happiness need not be affected by lousy fortune or problems as it is only your reaction which matters. By principle, a stoic is unfazed by both positive and negative situations, as they are only involved in their own orderly and virtuous response to each case.

2.2 Techniques for Strengthen Self-Discipline

It is essential to be aware of this. Understand the value of your life of self-discipline. You will be more persuaded of a need to make appropriate changes in your life when you are mindful of your undisciplined actions and their consequences. Feeling laziness, the urge to overindulge or the desire to give up or stop what you're doing is human nature. Despite all of these, you will make an effort to behave and act following your decisions. If required, seek professional advice and perform simple exercises to improve your self-discipline. Focus on Changing Your Identity, Not Your Behaviour. It's easy to think that trying to regulate your behaviour is about self-discipline. And while that's the primary objective, it's not the most effective way of thinking about it. You should instead concentrate on transforming your personality. This comes from a phenomenon called "habits based on identity." The theory is, if you want to change what you are doing, you have to change who you are first. If you can change your personality, so changing your behaviour will be much easier. Let's say you're going to eat less junk food so you can lose weight, for example. You're at a birthday party, and somebody offers a slice of cake for you. You could say, "No, thanks, I'm trying to lose weight." That's a perfectly valid answer, but it's based on self-denial. You are still the kind of person who is eating cake; this time around, you're just trying to say no to it. This can made you feel bad if you are doing enough. And with time, you would probably say, "Screw it," and just eat the cake. But let's look at how that similar situation plays out when you say, "No thanks, I don't eat cake," instead. It's a slight difference, but the emphasis shift is essential. Now you're asserting your new personality, rather than refusing yourself. Why is that strategy working? Thanks to something called "consistency bias." It's a word used by psychologists to explain our propensity to act in a way that is compatible with our personality, even if it makes no sense to do so. This propensity in many situations is harmful to our health. But if you're trying to alter your attitude, you should take advantage of that.

Remind Yourself Why You're Disciplined. It's beautiful to want to learn self-discipline, but why do you do it first? If it's just for your benefit, you're unable to stick by the stress and discomfort that will emerge as you develop your muscle discipline. Instead, I suggest that you have a specific reason. What change in your life will bring about better self-discipline?

You might want to tolerate junk food, stop smoking, or consume limited alcohol. You may want to work out more frequently or eat better to get more energy. Or maybe you want to learn a new skill at the discipline. You need to express it, no matter what the reason. And once you've done that, you have to remind yourself of your "why continually." It is recommended to write down your purpose on a sticky note, so keeping it wherever you see it every day. Here are a few areas to consider: Next to your bed by your monitor on your fridge your bathroom mirror your front door this way, you'll have a constant reminder of why you're trying to improve your self-discipline. If you can see the "why," it becomes much easier to let your feelings (instead of your emotions) guide your actions. Embrace Discomfort Just as you build muscle by lifting weights regularly, the more you exercise it, the stronger the self-disciplining muscles get. Regular practice is proposed to exercise the muscles of self-discipline that will drive you out of your routine and accustom you to escape the easiest route.

Here are a few routine self-discipline exercises you can do:

Take cold showers Take the stairs rather than the elevator Set up for an early workout class (preferably one that costs money, add some additional incentive) Walk or bike for chores instead of driving Read a book instead of watching TV.

Self-discipline can also be developed by doing some kind of exercise every morning. This usually means a long bicycle ride or rock climbing. But as understandable as some strength training or a long walk, it could also be.

The specific task doesn't matter; the idea is to start each day regularly with something that makes me a little nervous but is ultimately satisfying.

Whatever you do, just do it regularly and make sure it is uncomfortable (but not painful or dangerous) at least a little bit.

Focus on Fundamentals First

If you are attempting to build self-discipline, ensure that you don't forget the fundamentals. Precisely, you need to take care of your biological principles: Sleep Food Exercise These areas are easy to ignore in pursuit of other goals, but if you're sleep-deprived, hungry, and lack regular exercise, anything else you do will be more challenging. What's that for? The part of your brain that controls the functioning of executives (which regulates your wishes and impulses) requires sufficient energy and rest to function at its height. Strength comes from physical exercise and proper diet, while rest comes from sleeping.

Remember: Your brain is not separated from your body by some magical conceptual object. It is just as much a biological system as the bones, muscles, and gastrointestinal tract. If you don't give it the energy it needs and rest, then you're setting up for failure.

Try Meditation

What if someone told you that, while focusing on your breath, the key to improving your self-discipline was sitting still a few minutes a day? It sounds crazy, but some proper research shows that daily meditation can enhance self-discipline. Some researchers found in a study that completing meditation training increased awareness, boosted satisfaction, and enhanced emotional regulation. This points to meditation as a promising technique to encourage your self-discipline, as it is essential to regulate your emotions in line with your thoughts (as opposed to your feelings). There are plenty of aspects you can start meditating. You can try the Headspace app, which offers regular guided meditations for stuff like stress relief and attention boosting. But, perhaps the easiest method is just to sit down for a few minutes with your eyes closed and concentrate on your breathing. Practice getting your focus into your breath as your mind wanders. The workout at first seems dull and meaningless. But if you do it regularly, avoiding the impulses and cravings will be much easier.

Practice Building New Habits

Habits are distinct from self-discipline (and more necessary to change your behaviour, in many cases). But building a new habit is an excellent practice to develop self-discipline. Because you haven't built up the pattern yet, you must practice self-discipline to resolve the obstacle to doing so. The product of constructing new patterns is a win-win, then. You get to build a new model that directly benefits your life, and you get the secondary benefit of higher self-discipline. It creates a virtuous cycle, which makes any new habit more comfortable to maintain as your self-discipline grows. So what habit should you begin with? If your main goal is to build up self-discipline doesn't matter. But there are some good habits that everyone should have; here are some to continue with: Exercising regularly Make yourself a healthy meal every morning Drinking water throughout the day Having 7 –8 hours of sleep each night Flossing once a day Meditating for 3 minutes each morning Reading for 30 minutes per day Don't try to build all these habits at once; that's a recipe for failure. Start with one, focus on it for a few weeks, and move on to a new practice only once the existing habit has inevitably become.

Use Technology to Your Advantage

Although self-discipline is mostly an internal thing, technology can also be used to make it easier to develop self-discipline (or eliminate the need for it).

One of the easiest ways to do that is to install an app that blocks blogs, video games, and other enticing items on your computer or phone from being disturbed.

Although you may even use the "Screen Time" settings built to your phone, whether you need to move on to more important work or also if your electronics keep you from going to bed at a decent time, this approach works well. You can use a habit tracking app to retain self-discipline while you are building a habit. Eventually, you may be able to use technology to drive something through cravings. Let's say you are craving ice cream, for example. Instead of telling yourself, "You can't have ice cream," you can reframe the problem by setting a 30-minute timer on your screen. You can then inform yourself you can have an ice cream... once the timer is up. Generally speaking, 30 minutes is enough time for you to distract yourself and forget what you initially craved. This may not work for everyone (especially if you want anything highly addictive like a cigarette), but it is a strategy that will be found useful.

Embrace Imperfection

You are not going to be disciplined all the time, no matter how much you train. There will be times where you can't resist the lure, when you've had a crummy day, and when you give in to your urge to indulge in a cookie or miss exercise. Instead of punishing yourself when your patience is running out, you should forgive yourself and understand that this is a normal part of life. The aim is not perfection.

2.3 Pillars of Self-Discipline

There are some pillars of self-discipline:

- Acceptance
- Willpower
- Hard work
- Industry
- Persistence

Let's discuss about these pillars.

Acceptance.

Acceptance means that regarding self-discipline, you look at your life and asses where you stand right now. It is best to look at each area of our lives individually as in some areas we may be quite structured and in others less so. Identify the most critical areas, as well as your best. How controlled do you feel about your nutrition? Do you have a clean and beautiful desk and work atmosphere? Would you get sufficient physical activity? Do you work the whole time that you're at work? Must you try educating yourself in your profession? When we get what we want now, we could only strengthen. Once we acknowledge that in some ways we don't have self-discipline, it's challenging to move forward. When we realize where we are, we may make an actual plan for each field of our life to strengthen our self-discipline.

Willpower

Willpower helps us to break beyond our comfort zone and make it necessary to change this for the better, improve our life. The problem with willpower is that we only have a limited amount of it. You may have experienced yourself when you were going on a diet. A few days, you managed to stick with it, then you went back to eating the old habits. Your willpower has started to wear off. That's why the strategic use of our will power is significant. Willpower is like a self-disciplined spearhead. It's instrumental, but we have only a limited amount. That's why it's important to establish our environment in a way that requires as little effort as needed. If you want to go on a diet, throw out of your fridge all your junk food, so you don't have to waste your willingness to resist eating that cupcake. Prepare safe means the whole week in advance. This way, dieting will be accessible when you open the refrigerator with the right meals already waiting for you there. You are only going to use willpower to cook the meals and plan to go on a diet. It's also wise not to burden yourself with too many changes of habit at once. Take one practice of it at the time. Don't try to stop smoking, get fit, improve your education, cut your life down on television all at once. That is going to be too hard. Taking one habit at the time and make efficient use of your will power.

Hard Work

You have to know that if you want to be successful in life, there's no hard way around. You may get rewarded once in a while but hard work is necessary for lasting success. Hard work is a work which challenges you physically as well as mentally. Hard work makes you stronger, as you continually push yourself to the boundaries and expand. Improve hard work and your self-discipline will be significantly improved too. Through hard work, instead of being a passive observer, you take a driver's seat in your life and go wherever life takes you by itself. You might be okay to just go with the flow, but maybe you're not okay with where that ultimately makes you, like getting broken or sick. All in life, being in shape to being educated, content in relationships, and running a successful business, requires hard work. You will manage to push through any obstacle when you have a purpose in life, and hard work is more comfortable if you have a strong enough reason.

Industry

Industry means to put in the hours. Doing the work that needs to be done. It's not the same as working hard. Hard work does a challenging task, but you can do the easy task, too. Of example, you need to prepare the healthy food if you want to go on a diet. That's not particularly challenging if you learn how to do it, but it takes time, and because it's easy, people often just eat a snack bar. The industry is going to do the job, but it's not going to tell you what to do. That's why it's essential to know where you're now and where you're going.

Persistence

Persistence is when you get tired of doing the hard work but still work hard. Only if you have a clear purpose, can that be done? Whether you reach your goals is hard work. That's why you want to achieve them, and if you have a clear vision, you get there with perseverance. That doesn't mean that for decades you need to be stubborn and stick to your goals. Be wise, people change their expectations too, but you have to keep pushing forward when you have a clear vision and strategy on how to get there.

Persistence would create a positive cycle of its own. You start getting results when you are working hard on your goals. Such findings will provide you with more incentive to continue working hard to generate more results that will give you even more motivation. Look at these pillars in your own life and find out who is the weakest. Then work to make things better. Gradually, instead of another move.

2.4 Developing Daily Habits for Programming Mind

Because so much of what we do every day is driven by habits, cultivating the right habits will help instil the right amount of discipline in our lives.

But where are habits coming from, and how are they being developed? And why do we only follow through for so long before we give up and return to our old ways when we try to change our habits by either breaking bad habits or building good habits?

The biggest problem is the neural pathways that have been ingrained in our brains, particularly with behaviours that we've had for years and even decades. Neural pathways help connect neural networks to perform a specific function, such as walking up the stairs, smoking a cigarette, or in some way, preparing a cup of coffee.

Neural pathways help optimize behaviour, which is repeated continuously to reduce the mind's conscious-processing power. It helps the brain to concentrate on other potentially occurring things. It comes from our early days as human beings and is part of our genetic makeup, allowing for a more powerful mind that can be used to many other tasks rather than mundane things. However, in most situations, it is the seemingly ordinary habits that are repeated that work to hold us back. We seem to have more bad habits that affect our lives than good practices that help move us forward. Because these neural pathways are formed deeper and deeper over time, it becomes more and more challenging to break bad habits or even make good ones when the bad ones get in the way. Yet, if you can instil in your life the following patterns, you'll find that disciplining yourself becomes far easier. It's not going to happen overnight. Keep in mind that habits take time to form and break. But if you start small and build, you're not going to wonder how you can discipline yourself any longer, because you're going to embody the specific habits that promote self-discipline in life.

Gratitude

We're spending far too much time wanting things. The habit of appreciation helps move us away from wanting desperately what we don't have and towards appreciating what we do. Some incredible changes start to occur when we do this.

Gratitude's results are far-reaching. Recognition can do so much, from strengthening our mental health to our physical wellbeing and our spirituality. Most significantly, though, it helps move us away from a state of scarcity and towards an abundance of environment.

When we live in a depressed state, focusing on being disciplined and achieving our goals becomes quite impossible. We use so much of our mental ability to think about what we don't have and live in a state of dread that we forget what we do.

The state of absence translates into physical agony. This creates stress and releases stress hormones such as cortisol and epinephrine that affect a variety of our body systems. When we are in tension, our digestive, reproductive, and immune systems are all affected. Spend 10 minutes writing out all of the stuff you're thankful for every day. Even if you feel that you don't have anything to ask for, find anything. Check and see.

Forgiveness

If we spend a large part of our days in a state of anger, remorse, or embarrassment, we create more problems than solving them. Hate and vengeance absorb much more strength than forgiveness and love. We learn to let go of other things as we forgive.

We couldn't maintain self-discipline without the practice of forgiving. We're too concerned about how somebody wronged us even to concentrate on control or achieve our goals. Learn to forgive them if somebody harms you. It doesn't mean you have to forget automatically. Just forgive this negative energy and release it back into the world.

We let go of resentment by forgiving, which zaps our capacity to be self-disciplined. Forgiveness is one of the significant ways if you want to know how to discipline yourself. While at first glance, it may not seem like a discipline habit, it is one of the most significant that exists. Think of all the people with whom you are upset or who have wronged you, and write down why you forgive them. Try putting yourself in her shoes. In their case, what would you have done? Try to find certain humour within it. In everything that happened, try to find a lesson learned. I know firsthand how difficult it is to forgive some people, especially those who have done me a real wrong in life. But it was not until I let go of all those sensations of disappointment and anger that things started to change. I was so worried and stressed that I didn't push ahead.

Meditation

Meditation helps to bring peace to our minds. It gives us spiritual centeredness, which acts as an avenue of development. As we meditate, we balance out the noise and remember we are just one of the very many related beings in this world.

Meditation also influences our capacity to be self-disciplined. It clears the palette of the mind and sets the right tone for the day. This helps improve our mental, emotional, physical, and spiritual wellbeing all at once, helping you to reap some of the most important benefits for the smallest amount of time spent. It doesn't take long to meditate. It can take 10 to 15 minutes to make it. Keep your mind steady, and let it not wander. If it starts roaming, then reel it in. Keep your energies rooted in the earth, open your hands to face the heavens, and keep the air moving inside and outside of the lungs. Meditation is about our physical bodies being associated with those of our astral or spiritual bodies. When we can balance the two, we can lead a more cantered life without having to think about the daily things that tend to weigh down on us. This helps make our charge lighter.

Active Goal Setting

You set goals in your mind with an inactive target setting. They're passive, so concrete details are missing. You didn't define them accurately, and they exist in the abstract.

Different active targets. These are set out with specific goals. Their sense is profound. They're concrete and measurable. And you've got a plan for their achievement. It is much easier to achieve our dreams when we set long-term goals in this way and also engage in active goal setting daily. The active setting of goals instils discipline, as it gives us direction. It also helps us prevent problems by seeing what needs to be done on a specific day. Despite ambitious objectives, we're left in stormy seas like a ship without a sail.

First, you need to set some long-term goals to set moving targets. If you are with long-term goals, then you need to commit to setting and planning purposes monthly, weekly, and daily. And you must always keep a diligent track of your progress towards your goals. You can see with tracking and analysis how far you have come, where you are, and how now you have left to go. It's far harder to get distracted because before your very eyes, and you can see the impact there. And your subconscious mind can find fewer ways to lie to you or help conceal the truth from you. Create some daily goals for yourself each morning and identify the essential tasks that need to be done in the daytime, and then, so to speak, chase the frog.

Eat Healthily

Most people are not observing that the human body spends a significant portion of its energy processing and digestion of food (10-25 percent). The body uses more energy to digest the menu when the diet is abundant in carbohydrates, fats, and even proteins, some of which are primarily useless for us. Raw foods and fruits provide the most considerable boost to energy because they need less energy to process and, after the fact, offer more power for use. This is also referred to as improved Food Thermic Effect (TEF) or Dietary Induced Thermogenesis (DIT).The amount of energy that we have plays a big part in how cantered we are. When we're focused, discipline will help us achieve our goals. When we're too unconscious out of the food we've got, that's far more difficult to achieve. We spend the majority of our time feeling too tired to do anything. It's necessary not only to eat a healthy breakfast but also to eat healthy all day long. You need to prepare your meals to do this, and break those bad habits. When you eat fast food every day, you won't have the energy to be actively meeting your goals or have the willpower to follow through. Food can change the neurochemical makeup of the brain and has a significant influence on the connection between the mind and the body. If you can and limit your sugar consumption, go for raw, balanced, and organic foods.

Sleep

Sleep is directly connected with our ability to discipline ourselves. And getting the right amount of shuteye is a vital precondition for doing anything. If we don't get enough sleep, this will affect our mood, concentrating capacity, decision, diet, and overall health. If we speak of chronic sleep deprivation, the sort that affects a lot of people, things get even worse. Studies show that people who are regularly deprived of the right amount of sleep are at a higher risk for certain diseases. The lack of sleep has a considerable impact on our immune system. It is important to be sleeping for at least 6 hours, no matter what. Try not to drink too much caffeine at least 5 hours before bedtime so that your natural sleep cycle is not disrupted. If it can be done, stay away from too many contaminants throughout the day, such as alcohol, cigarettes, or prescription medicine. The benefits of getting enough sleep are substantial overall. Apart from helping you become more focused, it will strengthen your memory, curb inflammation and pain, reduce stress, inspire your imagination, increase your grades, sharpen your concentration, help you avoid depression, and decrease the chances of injuries.

Exercise

Exercising is a behaviour with keystones. This serves as a key to a life full of useful and healthy habits and free of bad habits. Do you want to learn how to discipline yourself? Instil the habit of exercise on keystone in your morning routine cannot begin to express the benefits of exercise. I spoke to several blogs and books I read about it. Yet, then again, many people pride themselves on the positive benefits of exercise. Yet not everyone in their lives makes exercise a priority. Why not, then?

While many people are busy rushing about, trying to get things done in the afternoon, when they do not work out, they fail to take the bull by the horn. Most people believe they can't develop the habit because they have too much to do without thinking about, rather than exercise. Okay, this is where a lot of people are wrong. Not only can you become more disciplined by infusing the keystone practice of exercise, but you can also improve your life in several ways. Firstly, activity decreases the stress and pain rates by releasing endorphins and neurotransmitters like dopamine and serotonin.

Furthermore, exercise improves health by increasing the blood flow and oxygenation of cells in the body, helping to fight diseases, and boost the immune system. So exercise naturally increases our ability to concentrate on the task at hand, allowing us to live a more disciplined life. Start small to instil the daily habit of exercise in your life. Continue with a 5 minute morning walk around the block. Only five minutes. Do that just for a week. Then, raise it to 10 minutes and do it for a week. And the pattern continues. Exercising will finally become a full-blown habit.

Organizing

To be self-disciplined and achieve our goals, we need to be organized. The organization is a practice that needs to be fully expressed, not just in your professional life but in your personal life as well. It involves arranging your home and office things along with the objects in your mind. An organized life is a life of the order. If you mark yourself as totally scattered, start small. Start by arranging a little space each day. For starters, organize your desk drawer first. Move on to arranging the bathroom medicine cabinet the next day. And so forth. To improve your organization, do one small thing a day. That is all that it takes. Like all other habits, an organization's obsession can be built up slowly over time. It requires some effort and attention, yes, but in the long run, it will be paying off enormously. Once you organize the physical space around you, the mind becomes more relaxed, more stress-free, and more able to focus. Besides, as your life is more organized, you can become more self-disciplined. It includes keeping lists and arranging the drawers together. When you're done using something, put it back in the position it belongs to instead of just throwing it out. It's the little things we do every day that have a significant impact on the quality of our lives. Pay attention to the little things, and you're going to reap substantial benefits.

2.5 Self-Discipline Exercises

It can help you become more self-disciplined at work to make small actions a habit. Although not all of these may be directly linked to your on-the-job or duties, they will support your efforts to maintain a mental discipline.

You should try to include several exercises into your schedule:

- Meditate for some time a day
- Make your bed
- Eliminate distractions
- Practice gratitude
- Revisit your goals regularly
- Remember that failure is part of succeeding

Meditate for Some time a Day

Meditation is an everyday self-discipline activity that is easy to integrate into your daily routine. Meditation also reduces stress and increases focus — both necessary to achieve realistic career goals.

Make Your Bed

You start the day by accomplishing a task before you get to work when you make the bed first thing in the morning. Before commencing your day, the feeling of a small accomplishment can produce a more productive and disciplined state of mind.

Eliminate Distractions

Make it a point when you are at work to avoid distractions that take time off working towards your goals. This may include small actions, such as putting your phone in your desk drawer, using a social media monitor or blocker, or simply blocking your calendar for a certain amount of time to concentrate on a job. By having a set schedule, maintaining a clean workspace, and getting enough sleep each night, you can also eliminate distractions. It may also be helpful to add useful distractions, such as listening to background music to help you tune out office noises— choosing whatever works best for you.

Practice Gratitude

Taking time throughout your day to appreciate small wins or points of happiness will help you improve and sustain motivation. You may consider making it a habit to write down at the end of each day, three things for which you are grateful. Remember, if at all, how the self-discipline and motivation were affected after six weeks of this exercise.

Revisit Your Goals Regularly

Keeping your goals visible can be an excellent motivator to work towards increased self-discipline. Write down your goals and display them on your desk or computer. Make time to celebrate small wins or surpassing key milestones.

Remember That Failure Is Part Of Succeeding.

Self-discipline does not necessarily require perfection. You're going to fail or fall short of setting patterns or achieving goals, and that's perfect. Failure is a natural part of the performance. The idea is to keep moving forward and to get closer to your objectives. Recognize the shortcomings, praise the successes, and don't give up. Honing self-discipline is a challenge, but it can help you move on to the next task by doing simple workouts, eliminating repetitive behaviours, and becoming disciplined in one single area. Start small and settle into daily habits, which will make you feel accomplished.

Chapter 3 Importance of Self-Discipline in Childhood

Self-discipline helps to promote judgment and an opportunity to inspire your child to make better choices. Children are not born with self-discipline, of course. They hear it from the people who are most prominent in their lives. One of the child's main advantage of learning self-discipline is that they are much more likely to grow up with more faith in themselves. They know, in difficult circumstances, they can manage themselves. A healthy self-disciplined child is also a child who can take on more complicated tasks. Unfortunately, these are great qualities of life to learn in any age! Your techniques in discipline should not be about regulating your child. Instead, it should be about telling your children how to control themselves. Children learning self-discipline will be better trained to face the challenges of life, handle stress, and live a healthy lifestyle even if you're not around. It doesn't necessarily imply that he has self-discipline only because a kid is well-behaved. Self-disciplined children may choose to give up instant gratification. They're able to make the right decisions no matter how they feel. Children with self-discipline can communicate healthily with intense emotions. They have learned the skills of managing anger and can also control carelessness. If adults correct them, they should respond politely, and they can take responsibility for their conduct.

3.1 Childhood Emotional Neglect

Emotional neglect in childhood is an inability of parents or careers to return to the emotional needs of a child. Such a form of negligence can have long-term, almost instant, as well as short-term effects.

It's essential for parents, teachers, caregivers, and more to understand why childhood neglect happens. It is also good to know what a child who experiences it looks like, and what can be done to fix it or help a child resolve it.

Continue reading to find out why this is happening during upbringing, and what it means for adult life.

What is childhood emotional neglect?

Childhood emotional neglect happens when the parent or parents of a child fails to respond appropriately to the psychological needs of their child. Mental neglect isn't inherently emotional abuse in childhood. Damage is often intentional; behaving detrimentally is a purposive decision. While emotional neglect may be a deliberate disregard for a child's feelings, it may also be a failure to deliver or consider the emotional needs of a child. Parents who do not care about their children emotionally would still provide care and essentials. They just miss this one key support area or mishandle it.

An example of emotional neglect is a kid who tells his or her parents that they are sad about a school friend. Instead of responding and assisting the child cope, the parent ignores it as a childhood game. The child starts realizing over time that its emotional needs are not essential. They are merely refusing to seek assistance. The consequences of childhood emotional neglect can be rather subtle. Parents can find it hard to realize they are doing it. Similarly, it may be hard for careers to understand the early warning signs. Extreme cases are more comfortable to identify and can draw the most exceptional exposure. Less extreme ones could be ignored.

Knowing the signs of childhood emotional neglect can be crucial in getting support from the child and parents.

How does emotional neglect affect children?

Symptoms of emotional neglect in childhood can vary from subtle to clear. At first, much of the damage caused by emotional negligence is obscured. Nevertheless, the effects can begin to show up over time.

The most common symptoms of childhood emotional neglect include:

- Depression
- Anxiety
- Apathy
- Inability To Succeed
- Hyperactivity
- Violence
- Developmental Delays
- Poor Self-Esteem
- Abuse of The Drug
- Isolation From Social Activities
- Uncaring or Indifferent Behavior
- Disowning Emotional Closeness Or Interaction

How does childhood neglect affect adults?

Those who are abused emotionally as children grow up to be adolescents who will always deal with the consequences. If their emotional needs were not accepted as infants when they arise, they might not learn how to handle their emotions.

The most common consequences of childhood neglect in adults include:

- Post-Traumatic Stress Disorder
- Depression
- Mental Unavailability

- Increased Risk of Eating Disorder
- Shunning Affection
- Feeling Profound, Psychologically Defective
- Feeling Hollow
- Poor Self-Discipline
- Remorse And Shame
- Frustration And Violent Actions
- Trouble In Trusting others or Depending on Someone Else

If Parents may never have understood the importance of their own emotions, and may not know how to handle their children's feelings.

Effective treatment and awareness of their own neglect experiences will allow people of all ages to resolve the short-term effects of emotional neglect, and also prevent future complications.

What is the treatment for the effects of childhood neglect?

Emotional neglect therapy for children is generally the same, whether it's experienced as a child or viewed as an adult who has been overlooked as a child.

The options for treatment include:

Therapy

A counsellor or therapist may help a child learn how to cope healthily with his or her feelings. If a child is used to block their emotions, recognizing and productively expressing emotions may be difficult.

Equally, years of ignoring feelings can lead to trouble expressing them for adults. Counsellors and psychologists may help both adults and children learn healthily to recognize, recognize, and express their emotions.

Family Therapy

If a child is emotionally abused at home, family therapy can help the parents as well as the child. A therapist can help parents understand their effects. This can also help the child learn how to deal with the issues which they may face. Early diagnosis can alter and correct attitudes that contribute to negligence and the possible consequences.

Parenting Classes

Parents who ignore the emotional needs of their child could advantage from classroom parenting. These lessons help parents and caretakers learn the skills needed to recognize, listen, and respond to the emotions of a child.

Mental neglect from childhood can harm the self-discipline and emotional health of a child. It taught them that their feelings do not matter. The effects of this ignorance can be severe and last a lifetime.

Treatment for emotional neglect in infancy may help children who have been abused to relieve feelings of loneliness and failure to control their emotions. Equally, parents can learn to react better to their kids and keep the process from happening again.

3.2 Importance of Teaching Self-Discipline

Self-Discipline in Student Life

Discipline can be described as an individual's ability to do a thing or perform a task within a pre-planned and pre-defined time frame. It is an individual's practice of best time management skills to accomplish the goals and complete the job promptly. Our lives are full of incidents of discipline.

We may experience the discipline in nature's work. An example of consistency is the sunrise and sunset at the precisely defined time. Moreover, the fall of days and nights, the seasonal exchange, and the death accompanying birth are the great examples of order in our existence.

Discipline plays an essential part in our lives. Excellent time management, productivity, and performance are indicative of a balanced life. There are few aspects of a focused experience, including; strict job preparation, carefully choosing targets, and remaining healthy and quick until objectives are met, and tasks are accomplished. Discipline is the cornerstone of worldwide success.

Discipline has a high value in students' life. It helps those to overcome failures, to ensure success and better planning for the future. There are significant benefits for the students to a balanced life. Discipline helps a student immensely in his academic success, first. On due time they do all of his work

A student understands the importance of his time better. And he makes an efficient strategy to make the best possible use of his time. He learns from his shortcomings and tries to overcome them to secure his success. Not only does he fail and excel himself, but he supports other students as well as his classmates.

He's suspicious of other teachers. He's still helping fellow students. His disciplined approach, therefore, awards him a reward. Through academic life, he is competent to target.

Second, in his non-academic life, the discipline holds great importance for a student. Not only does the training help him achieve his academic goals, but it also teaches him a way to be successful in practical life. A conscientious student is very mindful of his assignments. He becomes His parents' best friend.

He acknowledges their issues and is actively supporting his parents on their journey through life. He encourages other fellow-beings with discipline. He's just striving to be at his house, his friends, and his school best. The gift of restraint also profoundly shapes his personality. He encourages other fellow students to have their lives disciplined.

Third, the curriculum is of great value to students' future careers in their lives. A diligent student understands the importance of time and forward planning. He wisely selects the path he wants to go. He isn't disoriented, that is to say.

He appears committed to doing his job. He is working hard to get himself ready for his future career goals. A disciplined student knows precisely what things or works are essential to him to achieve what he wants to accomplish in the future. He's not gasping his breath. Therefore, unlike other students who don't have definite plans for the future, a disciplined student knows his achievements very well. Therefore, by practically applying discipline throughout his life, he is effective at achieving his career goals.

Discipline has been taught from the very beginning. It cannot be enforced immediately. It's our part and parcel of life. It is like a cycle that, over time, is becoming a more deep-seated habit in our lives. So it is necessary to help the child follow a disciplined life from the very beginning of life Discipline is very important in our lives. We need discipline in every step of our lives to become active. Life is disoriented and purposeless without control.

3.3 Ways to Teach Self-Discipline to Kids

No matter what type of discipline you use with your infant, your parenting approach will eventually strive to teach your child self-discipline.

Self-discipline helps children avoid gratification, resist undesirable temptations, and endure the pressure needed to achieve their long-term goals. Self-discipline is the key to helping children become responsible adults, from deciding to turn off the video game to focus on homework, to avoid an extra cookie while mom isn't looking.

It is essential to give children the tools they need to develop self-discipline and a chance to practice making good choices. Here are some things you can do to help your child learn and control themselves.

Provide Structure

Every day creates a similar schedule, and your child will become accustomed to the routine. Once she knows what she's going to do, she'll have less risk of being distracted by other events.

A good morning routine helps children know when to eat breakfast, comb their hair, brush their teeth, and get ready.

A successful after-school routine teaches children how to split their time between activities, homework, and fun. And a consistent method in bedtime will help children settle down and fall asleep more quickly.

Keep the routines of your child simple. And your child will learn, with practice, to follow the method without your help.

Explain the reason behind your rules

An authoritative approach is best when it comes to helping children learn how to make healthy choices because it makes them understand the reasons behind the laws.

Instead of saying, "Why I said so, do your homework now," clarify the underlying reason why statute. Say, "First, doing your homework is a good choice, and then having free time later as a reward for getting your work done." This helps them understand the underlying reasons for your rules. Your child may recognize the regulations serve a purpose rather than saying, "My mom said I've got to do this."

You do not, of course, want to launch long explanations or lectures that will annoy your child. But a quick comment on why you think those choices are relevant will help your child better understand opportunities.

Give Consequences

Natural consequences can sometimes teach some of the greatest lessons in life.

A kid who forgets to grab his jacket always when he races out of the door will not know if a parent still sends his coat to school. Facing the natural consequences of his actions (such as feeling cold during the recession) may help you remember to get your jacket next time.

Many times, children need to have logical consequences. A child who plays too harshly with his mother's computer will learn to be more careful when he loses privileges on his laptop. Or even a kid who seems to have difficulty waking up in the morning might need an earlier bedtime at night.

It's essential to avoid struggles overpower. It won't teach self-discipline to try to force your child to do something.

Say, "If you don't pick up your toys right away, you're going to have to go to time-out." Start with a penalty if he doesn't pick up, but don't yell or seek to comply.

Keep in mind that, by considering the potential consequences of his actions, he will learn how to make healthy decisions on his own.

Shape Behaviour One Step at a Time

Self-discipline is a process that takes years to refine and develop. Using methods of age-appropriate training to form actions one step at a time.

Instead of expecting a 6-year-old to be able to suddenly go through their entire morning routine without any reminders, use a picture chart on the wall representing someone who combs his hair, brushes his teeth and gets dressed. You can even take pictures of your child carrying out those tasks and make your map.

If appropriate, give your child reminders to look at the chart until he can look at the table and do each of the tasks on his own. He will likely need fewer reminders, and will not need the chart because his self-discipline increases.

Support him do that one small step at a time if your child is learning a new skill or gaining more independence

Praise Good Behaviour

Give positive attention and praise if your child shows self-discipline. Point out the more often you want to see good behaviour.

For example, rather than saying, "Good work doesn't hit your brother when you're angry," say, "Great work using your words to fix the problem." Often good behaviour goes unnoticed, and rewarding children for making the right decisions increases the probability that they'll replicate the behaviour.

Provide praise when children are doing something without having reminders. Say, "Great job sitting down before I even asked you to do your homework! "And' I am so proud that you have chosen to clean your room all by yourself today.' Just saying,' Great job putting your dish in the sink when you've eaten,' will inspire repeat performance.

Teach Problem-Solving Skills

Teach problem-solving skills and work together to solve different self-disciplinary issues.

A behaviour problem may be solved relatively only. A child struggling to get dressed in time for school may benefit from having their outfit picked out the previous night. Setting a five-minute timer might also hold her in the job.

More complex problems can involve a series of interventions of the form of trial and error.

A teenager who doesn't do his homework may need several changes before becoming more motivated to get his work done alone. Consider doing away with a right. If that doesn't fit, try to have him stay after school to see if he can do it before he's coming home. Keep trying different solutions until you can find something that works while keeping him involved in the process.

Model Self-Discipline

Children learn best through adult watching. If your child sees you procrastinating or opting to watch television instead of washing the dishes, he will pick up your habits.

Consider modelling self-discipline as a priority. Look out for situations where you may be struggling with discipline.

You might be spending too much money, overeating, or losing your temper when you're angry. Work on those areas and make it clear that you are trying to do better for your kids.

Reward Good Behaviour

A program of incentives can target specific issues with behaviour. A sticker map may inspire a pre-schooler who struggles to stay in his bed at night. An older child who is struggling to do his homework on time and accomplish his tasks will benefit from a token economy system.

Short-term reward systems should be in operation. When your child starts to gain self-discipline, phase them out.

Keep in mind that many bonuses do not cost money. Use extra privileges, such as time with electronics, to motivate your child to be more responsible.

3.4 Steps to Build Self-Discipline and Willpower in Students

The following are some steps that show How **to** Have Self-Discipline When You Study.

- Remove Temptations Eat Brain Food before You Begin
- Do Away With Perfect Timing
- Ask Yourself, "If I Had to, Could I?"
- Give Yourself a Break
- Give Yourself Rewards
- Start Small

Remove Temptations

If items that disturb you from your studies are out of reach, out of earshot, and out of the window, if possible, self-discipline is the easiest way. If you are tempted by external distractions, such as your cell phone, then turn the thing off entirely by all means. Nothing will occur throughout the 45 minutes you'll be sitting down to study (even for just a minute) that can't wait until you've got a scheduled break. If clutter drives you nuts, take the time to delete the clutter from your study area too. Unpaid bills, reminders of tasks you need to do, letters, or even pictures will grab your attention off your research, and when you try to learn, it doesn't belong in places

Eat Brain Food before You Begin

Research has shown that when we practice willpower (another word for self-discipline), our reservoirs of mental energy slowly drain themselves. Forcing ourselves to give up what we want in the now for what we wish to later literally zaps our glucose stores, which is the natural fuel for the brain. This is why we are more likely to head to the pantry for a chocolate chip cookie as we sit quietly, avoiding our cell phones than we would have if we were not practicing self-discipline at all. So, before we ever sit down to study, we must be sure to indulge in some brain foods such as scrambled eggs, a little bit of dark chocolate, perhaps even a jolt of caffeine to make sure our carbohydrate is constant enough not to drive us away from the learning we're trying to do.

Do Away With Perfect Timing

There's never a perfect time to start training for the exam. The more time you give yourself, the happier you're going to be, but if you sit around looking for the perfect moment to start learning, you're going to wait for the rest of your life. Your mates would ask you to go out to the movies to watch the final screening of the top film of the season. Your family members will need to be guided on orders or you will need your parents to finish cleaning up your room. If you wait until everything is right — when everything else is finished, and you're feeling great — you'll never find the time to learn.

Ask Yourself, "If I Had to, Could I?"

Imagine sitting down at your desk. There's an attacker behind you, with a pistol pointed at your head. If, as you said, the first and only thing among life and saying goodbye to the world was preparing for the next few hours (with scheduled breaks), could you do that? You could of course! Nothing in the world at that moment would mean more than your life. So, if you can do it then— drop everything and give everything you have in you to study — then you can do it in your bedroom or library's protection when the stakes are not that high. It's all about the force of mind. Say, "I've got to do this. It all depends on it."

Give Yourself a Break

In taking a break for yourself, we certainly don't mean abandoning all self-discipline and sitting in front of the TV. Strategically incorporate mini-breaks into your study session. Set a watch or timer for 45 minutes (not the phone that's switched off). Push yourself to prep for those 45 minutes and make sure nothing interferes with your job. Then, take a scheduled 5-to 7-minute break at 45 minutes. Use the toilet, stretch your legs, grab some brain food, reorganize, and when the break is over, get back to it.

Give Yourself Rewards

The key to being self-disciplined often lies like the reward you give yourself for willpower exercises. To many men, self-disciplining practice is a reward in and of itself. For others, particularly those who just try to learn to have some willpower while learning, something a little more practice will be needed. Set up a system of incentives, then. Set the timer. Practice 20 minutes training with no interruptions for that final. If you've gone that far, then make a point to yourself. Then, do it again, after a short break. If you do another 20 minutes, just give yourself a different position. You get your reward once you've earned three points— you've managed to study for a full hour without surrendering to distractions. Make the reward worth it and hold back the reward until you have achieved your goal!

Start Small

Self-discipline is not just natural. Many people are more self-disciplined than others. I have the remarkable ability to tell themselves "no" when they want to say "yes." Nevertheless, what you need to know is that self-discipline is an acquired skill. Just as the ability to make a flawless free-throw with a high percentage of accuracy falls on the court only after hours and hours, self-discipline comes from the regular practice of willpower.

It takes 10,000 hours to become an expert on something, but "You do not benefit from mechanical repetition, but by improving your results over and over to get closer to your target. You have to tweak the system by pressing, "he adds," allowing you to make more mistakes at first as you increase your limits. "So, if you really want to become an expert in self-discipline while learning, you don't just have to practice the skills, you have to start small, particularly if you give up to what you want now repeatedly instead of waiting for what you want most.

3.5 Secret of Raising a Self-Disciplined Child

Each parent wants to raise children who will be responsible adults one day. While the end goal is obvious; children who are capable of dealing with real-world problems, achieving goals, and living success. How that can be made is debatable. One suggestion is that we must teach self-discipline to children at an early age. Without breaking societal rules, children who are learned self-discipline can render decisions that benefit themselves and their objectives. What does it take for your child to foster self-discipline, though? Here are some strategies to raise self-disciplined children, which can be employed by any parent.

Set Firm Rules — and Expect Respect

Children who believe they can do whatever they feel like doing, and get whatever they want, tend to be the ones who respond when their demands are not met by crying or throwing a tantrum. "Children who understand clearly defined boundaries learn how to self-regulate and value limits.

Tell them why.You don't have to explain why you expect certain behaviors from your children. But if your child understands that your laws are based on simple criteria, they will recognize that they aren't arbitrary and are more likely to obey. For example, tell them, "You have to go to bed at night because your body requires a lot of sleep to stay strong and healthy." Or, "You have to put away your games so we'll know where to find them when you want to play next."

Offer lots of praise Whether it is making the bed, helping set the table, or letting his sister play with his blocks, make sure that by celebrating the successes of your child, you reinforce rule-following. "It's awesome that you followed the rule of making your bed. I'm so proud to act like a big boy!" or, "When you asked me for that crayon, you were so polite to say' please.' good work!"

Follow the rules yourself "Hanging your coat in the closet when you get home, putting your dirty dishes in the sink, not yelling when you're upset ... doing these things would show kids that just as they've got rules to obey, so do you.

Cultivate a conscience if a young child feels bad after not following the guideline, do not try to minimize his pain immediately. Feeling a bit of shame is an essential part of the learning process on how to distinguish right from the bad. Use it as an opportunity to teach; for example, "I know you feel bad. We are all making mistakes, but next time we're going to learn how to act.

Build Problem-Solving Skills

One of the main reasons kids have poorly behaved is because they feel frustrated and helpless. If you give kids the tools they need to figure things out on their own, they're going to behave better because they're going to be better equipped to take care of themselves and won't come to you crying or acting out each time they meet a challenge.

Let kids make decisions.

Give children the chance to make decisions when they're old enough to understand.

"What flavor drink do you want to take to school, when kids are able to make these small decisions, take a note: if your kid struggles with her sister, for example, instead of yelling "Don't do that!" or giving her a time-out, it is recommended to ask: "How can you treat your sister?

Encourage a "try, try again" attitude.

Of course, doing everything for them is much easier for you. Still, it's crucial to let preschoolers learn and thrive without your intervention — whether it's tying up their shoes, putting away toys, or organizing socks in the laundry.

Make them think things out.

Extend the cognitive abilities of your child by encouraging him to find answers for himself. For example, when your child asks a question about how to do something, you answer with your issue: "What do you think you should do?" Such an answer would ultimately give him confidence in his own ability to figure things out.

Help Kids Practice Patience

No-one, especially young children, likes to wait. Developmentally and neurologically, it's difficult because kids live by always letting their needs be known. That's why parents must begin teaching patients in the infancy years. You want your kids to gain tolerance for the often-uncomfortable feeling of impatience, so they won't misbehave or act impulsively in the future when faced with that feeling.

Make them wait.

Don't drop everything every time your child asks for something. Let your child feel the unpleasantness of waiting, as it is a great agent of change. For starters, by not immediately giving him the juice, you are going to help him get practice in handling his impatience.

Tell them what they're feeling.

Toddlers can't express their anger at having to wait for items, but when they demonstrate patience, you can support by marking their feelings and offering encouragement. If your pre-schooler will have to wait for his turn, you could say: "I know it's hard just to stand here, and you're doing a fantastic job. You're patient, and that's awesome!" It's more likely that when you affirm your child's frustration with something, he will try harder.

Engage in activities that promote patience.

Encourage your child to do activities that don't yield immediate results, such as building blocks and solving puzzles, or planting a flower seed and watching it grow over time. Make sure they don't just play with high-tech gadgets that offer instant press-of - a-button efficiency.

Put an Emphasis on Empathy

How many times did you have to referee a blow-up because your pre-schooler was stealing a gift from a friend or refusing to share it with her sister? Born children believe the world revolves around them. So the faster you help they understand that everyone has emotions and feelings, the less likely they will be to behave in ways that offend or harm others.

Celebrate your child's acts of kindness.

In general, naturally occurring ways to teach empathy are best found. If your child shows respect for another, with a straightforward narrative, you can reinforce her tendency. For example, if you see your small child with a blanket covering her doll, say, "It was so kind of you to make sure your dolly is warm and cosy. She had to be very cold.

Ask, don't tell.

To a kid, you can't explain empathy, but you can start getting her thinking about the feelings of other people. Kids of this age will not understand lectures but you can increase their awareness level if you ask them questions. For example, if your child isn't going to let her friend play with her stuffed animals ask, "How do you think your friend feels when you're not going to share your stuff?"

Help them read body language.

One of the fundamental ways we gain empathy is to be able to interpret the movements and facial expressions. Give your baby pointers: "See how your Aunt felt when you shared your cookie with her. Have you noticed that she was smiling? You made her feel so happy at first." Your baby may not fully understand at first, but when she does, she will be caught up in the reactions of others— and will be better able to see how her behaviour will affect others.

Last, you won't be able to teach your kids how to discipline themselves overnight. There will no doubt be moments when they misbehave, no matter how hard you have tried to prevent it. After all, they are kids. But if you keep focusing on those texts, the lessons will sooner or later sink in. Your well-behaved kid will need less and less input from you, as they do.

3.6 Self-Discipline Leads To School Success

Every parent wishes that their child will succeed in school, but it is not just success that happens. If you want to boost the success of your tween at school, you might want to think about promoting its self-discipline. Self-discipline is not only strongly related to school grades but also constructive school-related attitudes and preventing problem behaviours such as drug use.

Elements of Self-Discipline

Self-discipline is widely debated, but what do you know about it? When we are talking about "self-discipline," we are talking about several different factors of personality. Low impulsivity is one element of self-discipline. A child with low impulsiveness should wait their turn, avoid interrupting conversations with others and remain sitting and quiet when necessary. The ability to control one's own feelings, emotions, and actions often require self-discipline. Finally, an essential element of self-discipline is the ability of an infant to delay gratification. A child with a sharp delay in gratification skills may later reject a small, instant reward in return for a bigger prize.

Self-Discipline and Academics

Psychological studies have demonstrated that self-discipline is essential to academic success. For example, a 2005 survey of eighth graders showed that self-discipline was strongly associated with the marking period and final GPAs, test scores for student achievement, and admission into a competitive secondary school.

Self-Discipline and Problem Behaviours

Not only does self-discipline seem to be linked to academic success, but it also makes a child less likely to have disruptive habits that might interfere with school performance. In 2002, a group of psychologists tested the delay of gratification for middle school students by asking if they would like to receive $5 immediately or $7 a week later. Those who had been waiting for the $7 reward not only earned higher grades than their $5 peers, they were also less likely to have had school discipline problems and lower substance use rates.

In comparison to school, children with high self-discipline often behaved differently. In particular, they were less often absent, completed more homework hours, spent less time watching television, and started their homework earlier in the day compared to low self-disciplined students.

Children with a substantial gratification delay used marijuana, alcohol, and tobacco all less often than children who displayed a moderate gratification delay. Ironically, the researchers also found that higher self-esteem was correlated with the desire to expect a reward. In other words, self-discipline seems to be associated with many variables, which are critical to the success of the school.

The Importance of Self-Discipline beyond the Tween Years

Although we've concentrated on studies conducted with tweens here, self-discipline remains essential for academic and career success well beyond the inter-years. For example, the findings with respect to problem behaviours and grades were also repeated with students at high school. Furthermore, it has been found that college students with high self-discipline are more likely to be inducted into the prestigious Phi Beta Kappa honour society than peers with low self-discipline, even if they are similarly intellectually talented. All in all, promoting your child's self-discipline can now get a big payoff both far and down the road.

Chapter 4 Self-Discipline and Personality

Good intentions just don't compensate. If we want to change a bad habit, learn something new, or make a positive difference for others, then we need the self-discipline to be sufficient.

Self-discipline requires determination, self-control, commitment, effort, and stamina. There is a need for encouragement, as you just want to achieve your goal enough to choose to move forward. For example, it can be fuelled. Once children see adults inspired to try new things, prepare for success, make efforts, cope with failures, and celebrate success, they understand how important motivation is to achieve almost anything.

Stop, Think, and Make Good Choices take self-control. There will be a lot of decisions to make along the way to achieving a target. Some of them will be big decisions moving toward progress, while others will distract from the intended goal. That is how we all learn to self-control. We take advantage of good choices and suffer the consequences of bad ones, which should lead us to learn to Stop and Think always. Good Choices will come more easily over time.

The initiative is what will get us to do the task-at-hand. This encourages us to ask questions, ask answers, and try again when we are not happy. The initiative needs a positive and productive attitude towards work-the desire to move forward and find solutions or to discover opportunities. A strong sense of purpose motivates that.

Encouragement is the key to keeping kids working hard. Recognize and show appreciation for commitment (not perfection!), and you are going to get more and more. Talk to kids about trying something new, encourage them in the process, and help them see more initiative leading to better outcomes. Words of encouragement are helpful, such as: "Hang in there and stay positive!" "You are important to the team, so keep trying." "Continue to work on it, and you're going to improve!" Stamina is what keeps us moving in the right direction to succeed. This distinguishes between just trying and succeeding. In an age when so much is happening too quickly and seemingly straightforward, it can be hard for kids to learn the value of being steadfast and diligent while achieving a target. It takes more than words to encourage; it needs experience. At school, we approach big projects by breaking them down into smaller activities, creating a timetable and a rubric, directing completion one step at a time, bringing it all together, applying the finishing touches, and feeling the excitement of an excellent job!. Involve your kids at home in important projects-such as gardening-that require preparation, energy, and commitment to accomplish. They want to contribute in ways that benefit others and themselves. It's crucial for them to feel that they're adding to the family at home, their park squad, and their school class. Stamina, commitment, determination, self-control, and motivation are essential to discipline oneself.

4.1 Becoming a Disciplined Person

Self-discipline is a psychological pattern where you choose to do what you know you should do and not what you want to do. It is the inner force that drives you to exercise from the bed, rather than sleeping in. It is the affirmation of willpower over more fundamental desires and synonymous with self-control.

It includes having the initiative to get started and the endurance to persevere. Being disciplined gives you the strength to withstand difficulties and hardships, be they physical, emotional, or mental. This causes instant gratification to be overlooked to gain something better while taking time and effort. Discipline is one of the cornerstones of a successful and fulfilling life, and we should all strive to master something.

Benefits of becoming a disciplined person

When you are persistent in doing the things you know you're supposed to do, if you know you're supposed to do them, here are the advantages you'll enjoy:

- Attain your goals. When you do the things you know you should do regularly, the chances of achieving your goals will increase dramatically.
- You're going to skyrocket your self-esteem. You build up your self-confidence every time you force yourself to do something you think you should do.
- People will be highly respectful of you. It includes everyone who witnesses your efforts from your partner to your boss.
- You are going to influence people's lives. Every good and right thing you do has an impact on the lives of those who watch and can have a ripple effect on future generations.
- In every area of your life, you'll see greater success. You'll enjoy a life that is more satisfying and contenting.

The Downside of Lacking Discipline

If you repeatedly fail to do the things you know you ought to do, when they ought to be done, here's the downside:

- You won't achieve the goals. I've never met anyone who managed to make any worthwhile goal without discipline.
- You're not doing well with yourself. You know what's right and wrong, no matter how hard you try to justify your actions. It only makes it worse to lie to yourself.
- You'll lose respect for those who depend on your actions.

Deciding to be a disciplined person may prove to be one of your most important decisions because of its powerful influence on every part of your life.

A Commitment to Discipline

The first step to becoming a disciplined person is committing yourself that you will be doing the things you know you should do when you should do them from this day forward. You cannot allow yourself to make excuses as part of this contribution, or justify not doing what you should do. If you're struggling with discipline, just start small. It is how we all began. Start by removing the garbage that is overflowing, answering an email, changing the light bulb, or cleaning your bathroom. Continue doing all the little things you know you should be doing today, but don't feel like doing it. Becoming a person of discipline will probably be the most challenging thing you do, but it can also become the most rewarding. All successes are built upon the foundation of training in every part of your life. Anybody want to encourage you to start doing the little things you know you're supposed to do. Recognize yourself as you do, for everything you do. You can train yourself to become disciplined with constant awareness and a sustained effort. This is not the first time I blogged about the importance of discipline, and it's not going to be the last. Nothing has a higher dollar value to the market than the regulation of the more than 1000 little things on my list.

Discipline is one of the key differentiators that distinguish those who lead a successful life and those who do not.

Here Is Another Example Of Becoming A Disciplined Person:

Set your alarm clock to ring about twenty minutes earlier than the morning, usually, you wake up. Get off your bed immediately, without hesitation, when the alarm clock rings. This may be hard, but it's an excellent exercise to become a more disciplined person. As for making promises, be sure that you can fulfil your commitment before you write it. Making promises and not carrying them out isn't a good idea, as this tells the subconscious mind that you will never keep your promises. Make promises that are fair to yourself and others that you can fulfil. Beginning with simple promises, which are easier to fulfil, is better and wiser. It teaches the subconscious mind to keep its promises.

Another thing you can do is think about and find out what kind of habits you need to change and start working to improve them.

- Do you avoid talking with certain people? Talk to them.
- Do you continue your day by checking your inbox, reading the news, and performing small, unimportant tasks? Adjust your business order and continue your day with more important tasks.
- If you want to become a more disciplined person, you need to be severe and put time and effort into this task. You'll also need to do some drills to improve your ability and make it a habit.

Do not worry if you lack discipline. With a little training, you can improve it. You can learn to keep your promises, make commitments, and follow them out, and you can learn to achieve what you are attempting to be doing. You will learn to persevere and learn to make your life more disciplined don't want to go into this subject in-depth here, as I've written about it in many of my posts as well as in my novel, Strengthen Your Willpower and Self-Discipline.

4.2 Qualities of Self-Disciplined Person

Self-discipline resembles the Ultimate goal. If you can master that, you can do just about anything that you put in your sights. Discipline comes to us, at certain moments, more quickly than others. You are going to the gym daily, for example, before your big summer beach holidays. We have no issue with a certain level of discipline for a short time and with a very particular objective in mind. But there's still the big question. How do we maintain the way we live our discipline? Here are ten habits of highly disciplined people.

They Commit

Disciplined people are faithful to the word. It's set in stone once they decide to do something, and they don't even need to have an accountability partner to hold them on track.

They Avoid Temptation

It is so hard to avoid pressure, doesn't it? Well, what do you guess? It's challenging for everyone, and that also involves the highly professional person; it's not necessarily any better to resist temptations, it's better to avoid them altogether!

They Take Care of Themselves

Their body is its temple. Things such as sleep, healthy nutrition, and exercise are high on their list of items to do. They understand the impact these environments have on other aspects of their well-being, including attitude, work performance, and relationships.

They Work at Developing Habits

Many peoples perceive a controlled life as synonymous with an impoverished life. But they don't see it in that way. They see only that they gain a new behaviour, which requires time and energy to develop.

They Set Boundaries

To lead a disciplined life, you need to know your limitations, especially when it comes to your time. Setting boundaries and saying no to things you don't want to do or that are distractions makes room to accomplish what is essential and essential each day.

They Revel in Routine

Routine is the pillar of discipline, especially as far as productivity and time management are concerned. This can be done in a variety of ways, like running every day before even looking at emails so that you can continue the day with a clear and open mind.

They Lead with Their Mind over Their Mood

They're not letting their feelings — like not even being in the mood to go into the gym on any specified morning — get in the way of going. They just focus and stick to the routine.

They Live and Die by Deadlines

Their schedules are authoritarian. They don't just set goals; they use simple mini goals and achievements as indicators to keep themselves on track along the journey of life.

The famed marshmallow test is usually the most well-known test of discipline. Children were asked to sit in front of a marshmallow during the test, and provided them some choices Eat the marshmallow now or would get two if they could resist eating it! Highly self-disciplined people can pass up immediate gratification in the pursuit of more significant long-term gains.

4.3 Characteristic of Self-Discipline Achievers

Those who achieve their goals consistently programmed themselves to experience performance. They learned in self-discipline. While most people spend a weekend lounging in front of the TV set, the self-sustained is busy advancing his career or promoting his business.

To achieve the qualities of a self-disciplined accomplisher, you need to establish characteristics that are common to all achievers. These are as follows:

A Positive Outlook

Self-disciplined attainders don't blame anyone for their current condition. They are going out to Change them, alternatively. They look at that glimmer of hope always in darkest clouds. They are investigating how they can turn a terrible situation into some kind of gold mine. The negative minded person recognizes only an insurmountable hurdle, becomes depressed, and embraces his station in life.

Vision

If you don't see any hope in your future, you will continue to waste your creativity and your imagination. You drag into your private prison where the only thing that seems real is the bars that enclose you on all sides. The Achiever sees endless possibilities. The reasonable demands of life do not constrain him. After 40 years of employment, there is far more to his life than retirement, and little to show for it.

Strong Belief in Self

There are many well-meaning complainers out there who advise him to embrace his lot in life, but he refuses to listen. There, the attained knows were better things out there, and he can and will accomplish them.

A Strong Sense of Purpose

The Achiever isn't about to accept the status quo. He has something more in mind, and he's not about to abandon the fight to get what he wants because others are telling him he doesn't have the know-how, money, or the millions of other excuses they're throwing his way. Whatever it takes, his sense of purpose is pushing him to success.

Ability to Plan

The reason so many struggles to make their lives better and packed with excitement is because of their enplaning. They may have a specific goal in mind, but they go nowhere without a plan. It is not that they have no preparation capabilities. Many people are taking great pains to plan their holidays, a wedding, or build their own home; they just don't see that the same talent can be used to prepare their future!

New Skills

No-one knows everything. Education is a process that is constant and does not end once you have a diploma. The attainders head out to learn what he needs to know to turn his dream into reality to optimize its value. He likes to read. He takes lessons in writing or seeks a mentor who can give him the skills he wants.

Is Communicative

The Achiever is never alone, nor is he trying to do it all by himself. He works with his instructor, communicates with those "in the know" until he knows necessary to strike himself out.

Is Patient. Success never happens overnight too many people lookout to "get rich quick" and become disappointed when they find that they have to work to achieve success. This is particularly true of affiliate services. The misconception of easy money is firmly entrenched in the minds of potential affiliates. It's much easier to sign up for several programs in the expectation that one will deliver the quick income, then it's

Fighting For That Remaining Revenue

Understands the Value of Perseverance

If you are not willing to fight to achieve your goals, then the average life you're living right now is the perfect one for you.

A Sense of Pleasure

The achievement of any worthy goal should be something that Lights You Up! It should never become something of a drudgery. There should be a sense of real anticipation to start the day off and a sense of satisfaction, realizing that at the end of the day, you have moved a step closer to your goals.

4.4 Creating Internal Strength

Most people are aware of the need to improve themselves ongoing. But the focus is often put on external factors: physical fitness, learning expertise to become a stronger leader or executive acumen.

And none of that will get you where you want to go from a deep inner core without help.

Here are some tips for keeping up your strength throughout.

Ask Yourself, "Why?" Then Find Your Answer.

Some people avoid complacency and complacency most successfully when they have a reason when they can answer the Why question. The meaning of life is to find your ability.' You will discover the most significant strength when you have a reason you are doing your best work. That is when the willingness for something can go beyond the desire for protection. Needing to make a difference primarily comes down to the fear of failure. Focusing more on intent cultivates the power and drive to tackle setbacks.

Put Yourself First

Ultimately we do not think there is a real work/life balance. Having your well-being, your top priority will help you find the rhythm of life you can manage and hold. It's like filling up your well or putting on your mask with oxygen before trying to help another. Stress comes from thinking that you've got the resources and skills to manage the challenges of life. Give yourself time to build that equipment, and provide the tools to help guide your life. Feeling self-centred makes you a more significant contributor to your objectives, which ultimately provides a successful outcome to those in your sphere of influence who depend on your strength to progress.

Train your mental and emotional body, as well as your physical self.

Your body is stronger than you think, and if you need it, it will give you what you need, if you nourish it the right mindset. That's just as important as having the proper nutrients. A positive approach and a flat work rate will see you through even the ruggedness times.

Decide, commit, and act.

Being effective relies on energy-efficient usage. Indecisiveness diminishes strength and encourages a lack of cooperation, so it's a blessing you offer to yourself and others that you learn to be decisive.

Don't let the fear factor in your decision making.

Many people reject opportunities because of the fear that they may not be able to do it or that something may go wrong. Consideration of the pros and cons of our actions is known, but be self-conscious too. When fear prevents you from the next move, adventure, or obstacle, then you allow it to overthrow you. It makes you your own worst enemy, squandering your growth and growth.

Embrace what scares you

You will face immense challenges leading to increased confidence and self-confidence. Life can be a constant struggle between how much you think you hopefully won't do and what you can't do. Stress comes from doing what you didn't know you could. Change happens when you trade comfort for the challenge, and the outcome is a new, stronger you. It is fun and exciting.

De-clutter your mind.

Even as little as 10 minutes of relaxation a day does away with the mental garbage that depletes your strength. This brings back emphasis and clarity. The people meditating are one step ahead of others. Our minds move faster, and they are clear-minded and far more decisive. They are a reckonable force.

Become your own best friend.

People don't feel the need to spend time alone. The time was spent searching for oneself is psychologically nourishing, which gives us the power to do it over and over again.

Practice calm and self-control in adversity.

Aggression is eating away at energy and creativity, replacing it with aggression and closeness of thinking. Nervousness also weakens the soul, anxieties the mind, and forbids your light to glow through. Replace them with the calm, guided determination that will help you accomplish whatever you set out to achieve.

4.5 Factors That Affect Self-Discipline

Self-discipline is one of the essential requirements for achieving success, but too often, there is a lack of self-discipline.

A few of the reasons responsible for lack of self-discipline are:

- People are not born with the self-discipline; they need to develop it, but they don't know how to improve it.
- The mistaken idea that self-discipline is something challenging to achieve and requires so many misrepresentations.
- Negative mental programming and negative environment are also responsible for this lack of it.

- Laziness and lack of enough inner strength also prevent one from being more self-disciplined. In this situation, one avoids doing things that require effort and persistence.
- People prefer comfortable laziness, instead of actions that require effort. Laziness is convenient, since it is pleasant and effortless, while self-discipline involves effort.

Fear of failure

Is it also a reason for lack of self-discipline? It prevents initiative and perseverance and leads to a lack of inner strength.

Temptations weaken self-discipline.

Each day we are all subjected to many forms of temptation. We're subjected to advertisements in newspapers, magazines, and on television, asking us to purchase this or that. We see a wide array of products for sale in stores and shopping malls, and we are given a variety of ways to spend time, including television programs, movies, restaurants, concerts, sports competitions, and many other activities. How can you miss the supermarket's beautifully packaged and tasty food, or avoid watching a TV show that provides an enjoyable break from everyday life? Accepting all these pleasures indiscriminately and performing them without using common sense appears to undermine self-discipline.

Lack of self-esteem

Is another factor that leads to a lack of self-discipline?

Lack of goals or purpose in life

It is also responsible for the lack of self-discipline and vice versa.

Procrastination

Is another reason for lack of self-discipline?

A lack of self-discipline also causes a lack of willpower, motivation, and ambition.

A weak state of health

Might even lead to weakness in this critical ability.

These are just a few of the reasons for lack of self-discipline. This situation can be remedied, but few people know-how.

4.6 Lack of Self-Discipline

A common characteristic of personality is the enjoyment of the short term. So instead of waiting until the student has the knowledge of trading on a demo account or has completed a trading course that he would immediately start live trading, the lure of making easy money too high. Or they've completed an internship and the tutorial and then get upset over a loss. The student who does this tends to think about the immediate pain of gratification they can feel, rather than the bigger picture. Set long-term trading targets and imagine the feelings, benefits, incentives, and satisfaction were arising from these goals being achieved. This will drive and motivate you and focus your mind on achieving those goals away from the immediate and destructive short-term gains from your focus. Learning to project yourself emotionally into the future this way will help develop self-discipline and inspire you to do the things you need to do to be productive. Remember, what you do today will affect the rest of your life.

Seeking Pleasure/Avoiding Pain

How you observe both pain and pleasure has a significant impact on how you are or will become self-disciplined. As discussed earlier, the majority of traders are reluctant to pain that triggers adverse emotional exchange.

Self-discipline is about being in charge and planning when you are going to let yourself feel pleasure or pain. To do that, start doing things you dislike, first of all, making you feel uncomfortable. So offer yourself a reward by doing something that you then enjoy. Repeating this exercise daily will teach you not to stop doing things, and will build the ability to do more easily painful things. You must develop yourself in trading to comply with the rules of your trading strategy, although you may incur losses.

Being able to have a healthy life, it is essential to have a balance of pleasure and pain. Too much suffering, and you get immobilized because there's no incentive to help you. Too much happiness and you get immobilized because there is no incentive for you to experience the pain. Previous bad experiences will affect how well you're adjusting to a controlled lifestyle. Bad experiences with a particular task in the past can make it harder for you to be compliant because of previous extra pain. You will have a more balanced approach to the job by maintaining self-discipline by controlling these emotions by combining both pleasure and pain emotions with the task. Starting a task might be considered frustrating, but you will be inspired to start the job by thinking about what it feels like to have accomplished it.

There are Some Examples:

Procrastination

Procrastination relates to avoiding pain. This sometimes tends to be a painful and challenging process concerning not having the information needed to complete a task and the assumption that the job will, therefore, be. By concentrating on the advantages of fulfilling the responsibility instead of the pain, you will more positively perceive the mission that will encourage you to do something about it. By focusing on the pleasure of the future, you will overcome the current pain of the task.

Avoidance

People use prevention behaviour to prevent them from feeling the pain of doing something they have to do that they find inconvenient. Other activities are often used to replace the business that they should be doing, thereby avoiding pain. These eliminate behaviours are used in that fear of the other task they should complete, which may include fear of rejection, lack of motivation, or even success. They are irrational fears that are learned from past life experiences that prevent self-discipline by stopping the action needed to complete the task. By removing this fear by reintroducing activity and focusing on future benefits, you unblock the path to task action, and avoiding behaviour becomes a thing of the past.

Bad Habits

Habits are mental behaviours that reanimate, such as the way you think, or physical patterns like the way you behave. The practices are either healthy, they enrich your life, or they harm your life. While good habits will make you look good in some areas of your life, bad habits will keep you from progressing in some aspects of your life.

Self-discipline is about modifying your actions, and improving your bad habits can make you more self-disciplined. The behaviours are unconscious, and the subconscious mind regulates them. To change these habits, we need to be conscious of these habits and start thinking about why you are doing them. Nevertheless, patterns are familiar and comfortable and therefore appealing to us and become a part of who we are as human beings. Taking them away creates a feeling of anxiety and pain that contributes to psychological distress, and we often revert to the same habit. When this happens, the conscious mind gives in to the subconscious, and we feel powerless to resist. Habits are usually formed out of pain-avoidance behaviour. By applying a combination of punishment for bad behaviour and rewarding good practice, we will begin to change bad behaviour while promoting ethical conduct.

4.7 How to Become Self-Disciplined

It takes time and patience to learn how to be disciplined and a lot of hard work to get started. But every act of self-discipline also develops your self-esteem and confidence-vital for successful trading.

Start with small things like your environmental cleanliness and orderliness. Learning self-discipline in life's little things prepares the way for significant achievements. Those who are undisciplined in small matters are likely to be undisciplined in more pressing issues.

Following are some examples:

Reframing

As you get more self-disciplined, you could feel that you will be struggling to achieve your goals and goals. You will begin to develop a new, more positive perspective by seeing the' pain' that comes from a more balanced lifestyle as something other than pain. When looking at the bigger picture, you'll continue to see the suffering as helping your ambitions and objectives. Through putting things into a different context, e.g., negative to positive, you will find yourself more motivated and your ambitions and aspirations easier to achieve. Reframing also helps to deal with the results of learning. Begin to see errors as an experience of growth, rather than personal loss or setback.

Mental Visualization

Rather than the future, the subconscious tends to think about the next time. This is a natural evolutionary defence mechanism that helps us to be aware of the wild threat. As such, the mind tends to focus more on the discomfort than on the potential benefits of completing the task. It helps to reframe a mission by shifting the focus from immediate to the future. The best way to achieve that is through the visualization process.

The stronger you can imagine, feel the passion, and hear the sounds of achieving a mission or goal. The advantages and incentives associated with it, the stronger our motivation becomes to complete the task and reach the goal. Through shifting the focus of the pain to the reward, a mission can become a pleasurable thing to do, and our minds are much more focused on achieving our objectives. By changing your thoughts, you start changing your feelings, which will improve your actions in turn.

Rewards

The key to attempting to change bad habits and promoting actions enriching a good life is to be positive and consistent and have the right type of punishment and reward for each behaviour. You can generate good habits such as self-discipline by overcoming the discomfort of changing behaviours. To break bad habits, a mixture of reward and punishment is needed. If the incentives for the changed behaviour are delayed or sporadic, they can increase the reward value and become a greater incentive than if the reward is offered periodically.

Chapter 5 Self-Discipline in Life

The self-discipline is at the core of any successful person. Whether it's a success in their personal lives or their professional lives, it all starts with an inherent disciplined ability to self-control — your thoughts on that. Emotional thoughts. Behaviours. And your behaviour. You have to keep all of these in order.

To achieve the lofty goals you set, learning how to control yourself is a critical ingredient in the recipe for success. But there's nothing new about self-discipline. Indeed for thousands of years, self-discipline has been a topic of discussion. And some of the most famous people in the world have advocated that.

Referring to our ability to succeed in any attempt in life, "Good habits established in youth make all the difference." Without getting a grasp on our ability to control our behaviours and attitudes, we cannot develop such good habits.

What people have come to understand with success is that discipline is the gateway to achieving their goals. They tried to use regulation in their lives to make their dreams come true. Through developing a core set of good habits that helped them see things through, they leveraged the art of self-discipline.

5.1 Discipline Begins At Home

"There is wisdom in discipline" How to maintain that discipline? Have you ever thought of doing something to affirm discipline to yourself, your neighbour, and your fellow men for the development of our country?

A lot of students forgot to analyse good manners and ethical behaviour. Compared with before, youth usually have different methods of facing life. They're not afraid if they do that and this, what could happen to them. They're risk-taking people. Great, if they use it favourably, worse if it leads to their lifetime disappointment. We never think of any problems that could happen to them as long as they're happy. We have a compelling character that may fall into trouble at times. The reasons why they have that kind of personality because: first they're not correctly attended by their parents, parents don't even find time to be with their children, second, they're the result of a troubled family, a father with another family and so with the baby, third parents don't know what kind of mates their children have, fourth the type of setting they're in, and lastly because of technology.

Modern families don't teach their children self-discipline as a norm. External discipline, the one forcefully enforced by family and society, does not always convert into self-discipline. Modern societies do not, as a rule, teach their children self-discipline.

We can still hold guidance for next-generation parents in our heads, in our hearts, and our acts. They need to find time for the parents to be with their kids to develop a good relationship among them and their children. If they're at least busy earning a living, let them know they're precious to you, let them realize they're your jewels and treasures you're not going to lose. Early marriage is also a factor in why we have students who misbehaved, because even the parents don't know how to treat themselves. Kids were mishandled at the end. As they are not yet ready to create a family, they are going to decide to quit with a separate life. The outcome was deceptive and upsetting for their children to face the world without their guardians. Another consequence, the atmosphere quickly affects them. We need to know as parents who are our children's friends, are they good or bad. Another essential aspect that influences the students' actions is the technology that needs parental guidance. We need to learn what the technology's real function is, and that is to gain knowledge and improve their understanding.

Small, "innocent" acts of criminality can flourish and become complete-blown attacks on our society. Inside the home, martial law is not recommended, nor does physical punishment, unless truly necessary. Several well-placed buttocks smacks will damage the ego more than muscle and will receive the message loud and clear. The early active intervention will promote self-discipline, as children gradually integrate the notion that they are responsible for their actions and the protection of society as a whole. Discipline has to start from within, remember from ourselves that we are the boss of our soul whatever we do that we are responsible for. Through discipline, let's join our hands to have positive education, society, and the nation as a whole. You have your freedom to choose the kind of path that no one will be accused except you for wanting — no one but you.

5.2 Method for Gaining Self-Discipline in Everyday Life

We either know someone with remarkable self-discipline or have heard of them. They get up at 5 am, breathe profoundly and plan their day, run for six miles, and then drink a smoothie for breakfast with kale and protein. They're doing all of this before going to work at their start-up, which they're hoping to get in public next month. They're never wasting time, and their achievements are impressive.

Yet here you're talking, surfing the internet, reading online news, playing candy crush, and eating ice cream straight out of the tub from Ben & Jerry. Is this the life you want to live in? And, are you looking for an experience in which you will achieve your goals and dreams, whatever they maybe?

How can you develop the same kind of self-discipline others have? Discipline is key to a successful career, so are tricks available to help you become more self-disciplined? There is.

Here are some ways of helping you become more self-disciplined than you are now.

- Start Small Identify What You Want to Do Differently
- Remember You Are an Adult
- Make a List
- Make Choices in Advance
- Make Use of Technology
- Recognize Your Limited Temptation Capabilities
- Keep in mind that failure is always part of the success

Start Small

You don't have to wake up like a different person. People tend to make New Year's Day resolutions as a social event: They say this year will be different. Okay, this year, you can make it different, but you don't have to change it all at once. Pick just one thing for the best results. Otherwise, you can get confused with too many changes to make at once. It contradicts the desire to become a more self-disciplined human being.

Identify What You Want to Do Differently

Do you even like smoothies from the kale? Want to be? Although drinking one may seem to be doing the honourable, healthy thing, it is unlikely to make you a better person. Though, if you just do it for the wrong reasons, it may make you an insufferable jerk.

When you concentrate on fitness, choose something realistic, and that's going to make a real difference in your life, and hopefully, you're enjoying it. That might be going to the gym, walking up the stairs instead of taking the elevator, or restricting you're eating ice cream. Ask what would make a difference if you want to make your career different and more successful. Look at the performance of individuals with the job you want. What's unique from you? Are you arriving early? Dress up, even if it's a casual dress code? Will they reply within an hour to all of the emails? Find the features you lack, pick a significant one, and expand on that.

Remember You Are an Adult

Adults are not sitting around waiting for someone to tell them what they should do; they are just doing it. That may mean giving up some of your downtimes at work, but disciplined people are the ones this excels, and disciplined people expect you to keep going even if you choose not to. You can start small, once again. Set your phone timer for five minutes, if you usually sit at your desk and play on your phone before your manager comes along and gives you a new task. After that, when the alarm goes off, go and find your boss and ask for something new.

Make a List

Part of self-discipline is to realize what you have to do, and then do it. Sometimes you will struggle to come up with your next task when you're not used to behaving in a controlled manner. Start your day with a list of tasks that you'll need to do.

You should make the work-related tasks or schedule personal items part of your day. Everything can go on the list from emails to laundry, to a stop at the grocery store. Checking the things out of the agenda may help you develop self-discipline.

Make Choices in Advance

If your goal is to be mindful of meetings, then choose to leave your phone at your office.

Don't put it in your pocket, either. If it is not there, you can't play with it.

If you want to become more self-disciplined about food, ask the waitress to box half of your meal in front of you, or choose to eat just half of the sandwich at all times.

If you want to get on top of your emails, determine how many emails you will be responding to before you do anything else, whether it's five, ten, or all. Only decide before the situation arises, and you will find it much easier to stay active in the face of temptation.

Make Use of Technology

Technology makes people intoxicating — they can always check on Facebook or Twitter or Instagram, not to mention playing games and sending in friends. Yet technical tools can also help you build self-discipline.

You can also set timers limiting the amount of time you spend playing a game or on your favourite time-wasting website. You can use one that tracks your time to give you an idea of how you are spending it and then work from there to reduce the number of unproductive hours you spend.

Recognize Your Limited Temptation Capabilities

If it were easy to live a self-disciplined life, everybody would practice self-discipline. Yet, this is not so. Did you know, though, that any temptation you resist strengthens the ability to avoid the next compulsion? Thus, for example, you'll reduce the temptations when you make decisions in advance. That also holds for your personal life choices.

If you want to appear at the workplace holiday party sober and competent, decide in advance that you will be strictly limiting your alcohol intake. If you're going to eat healthily, go shopping at the grocery store when you're full and don't buy candy bags.

Find a way to make accessible the stuff you are dealing with less. That will reduce the number of times you're tempted to do something that damages your self-discipline. That will save your strength for unexpected temptations as well. When snacking on salty carbs, for example, is a nightmare for your diet, don't buy the potato chips.

When you know you're going to have a hard time discussing a particular topic with your boss without rolling your eyes and saying something rude back, decide what you're going to say beforehand. Instead, when you have the most energy against temptation, plan the conversation for the beginning of the day.

Remember That Failure Is Always Part of Succeeding

Most people want to become self-disciplined, and then they make the wrong decision on day two and give up on their hoped-for routine. You won't become organized entirely immediately, so expect some disappointment to occur along the way. Yet, if you're prepared for it, and you realize from time to time, you'll struggle. One mistake on your way to success won't derail your entire plan.

At the same time, you need to rejoice when you're having success. You have accomplished all five of the goals you set for yourself this week. Pay yourself back and celebrate in a way that will not diminish your success. Say your goal is to win new customers for your company. To take three days off from prospecting would be a poor reward. A successful compensation could include lunch with a friend at a fancy restaurant.

In all aspects of your life building, self-discipline will help. If you're ready to get started, pick one field and proceed.

Do not think about once about excellence in all aspects and do not worry about disappointment, just worry about getting better today than you were last week. Gradually, in that one place, you'll become disciplined, and then you can move on to another.

5.3 Self-Discipline: Key to Health and Wealth

Becoming Wealthy with Self-Discipline

All self-made entrepreneurs have familiar something: they have the right habits to help them make a difference. Essentially, applying the same patterns to our lives is the blueprint for how affluent can become. We have to ourselves to change our lives. Self-discipline means the effort that we make to do what we need to do, even if we are not in a mood to do it. There is no quick route around it, and without effort, there is no payoff. The amount of money we're making is equal to the importance we add to the world. And without the effort required, the value can't be increased.

We're going to discuss what all the wealthy people have in stock and what are the multi-millionaire strategies we should use to guide ourselves to success.

- All rich people have healthy habits
- They focus on continually improving themselves
- Every wealthy
- that kind of person has the best management skills
- Dreaming for big is also a key for how to become wealthy
- They strive to serve the people and make the world a better place
- Rich people always look for opportunities to expand their area of expertise

All rich people have healthy habits

A sharp mind and a healthy lifestyle always go hand in hand. If you don't consume the foods that provide nutritional value correctly, if you're not doing physical exercises to clear your mind, it's going to be very difficult to concentrate. The planet is brimming with obstacles and stress factors. It only adds more to your desire for money.

Getting more money is equal to getting your mind expanded.

There's a certain amount of wisdom and mental improvement needed to get a fortune. Not to mention the energy level, you'll need to produce hard work hours and hours. There was a no-brainer who will be essential to take care of your body, and even more significant than having to take care of your ledger.

You would also like to enjoy your cash after you've got it. You can only do that with a long and healthy life.

All wealthy people have the best time management skills

You will never see Bill Gates wasting time. Or any other billionaire. That is for a reason: time is more important than money. You can get more money, but you can't get more time. So it's very crucial to manage your activities properly.

Think about your daily schedule and on what do you use it.

On the point above we mentioned TV. Let's say that you watch TV for 2 hours every day, and you decide that you can use this time more productively. That will gain you: 2 hours x 7 = 14 hours/week. That is 56 hours a month. You just won more than two days by just removing a straightforward thing that you can live without. You can do a lot in these 56 hours, trust me.

Also, all the wealthy people are early birds. Most of them brag on how much they can work without sleeping. That's because they try to use their time as productive as possible. And with self-discipline and determination, you can achieve that level of efficiency also.

I don't say that you should become a workaholic, but being lazy is not a good idea either.

Dreaming big is the key for how to become wealthy

If you don't have a vision, you don't have a fortune. If you don't have that big dream that pulls you towards it, you will have to push yourself into doing something every day, and that's exhausting.

You have to have a big vision that you aspire to get. A big dream so compelling that it will make you jump out of bed right before that alarm starts to ring.

And if you are next to achieve your goal, make a new one right away. Without a vision, we just come to an end.

Dream BIG, live BIG!

They strive to serve the people and make the world a better place.

To get rich, you need to understand: life is not about "me" but about "we." Any company has the full function of serving the community and making the world a better place. And if you have no niche serving people, there's always room for charity. Compassion is one of the noblest feelings we can have, and it gives us proper respect for life. We cannot get that level of awareness anywhere else.

Live to help others is what is making our lives happy and fulfilled.

Whether you're a firefighter, boss, or cook, that doesn't matter. Your work is also valuable to others, and we are all accountable to each other. When we devote ourselves to improving the lives of other people, our lives become better. And our bank accounts, at the same time.

There's no chance that the wealthiest people on Earth are the most significant philanthropists, too.

Never settle down! It doesn't matter how much you do, and how good you are at what you're doing, there's always something to change. We need to move forward and grow to understand our potential fully continually.

Don't just become trapped in one place. There's no longer the time when we know, master something, and that's it. We have to be versatile, and we have to be able to play things up. What's popular on the marketplace now could go down in a month's history. If what you're doing goes downhill, you need to be versatile enough to move onto something else.

"Trees that don't bend with the wind won't last the storm."- Old Chinese proverb those aren't all the ingredients on how to get rich, but these are solid values that we need to follow in our lives to get there. Keep in mind that the amount of money we are getting is proportional to the value we are bringing to the world. And keep expanding and enhancing your goals and pursuing them. You are going to get in there!

Becoming Safe with Self-Discipline Did you know your wellbeing has a lot to do with self-discipline? It can help keep you healthier and safer.

In most people's minds, there is a misunderstanding about self-discipline. We equate it with poverty, harshness, and surrendering pleasures. You need to change the idea in your account if you think so too.

Continue to equate self-discipline with inner strength, bravery, inner strength, and not succumb to unhealthy behaviours, laziness, and procrastination. This ability will help you gain better control of your life, actions, and reactions.

Self-discipline can be of many ways to help preserve your safety. There is a lack of self-control, a lack of ability to set limits, and an inability to control unhealthy behaviours when it is absent. This preserves your health when present, however, and helps you stop doing something that could hurt your health.

Below, you will find several reasons why the possession of this skill is beneficial for your health.

- It Helps You Stop Eating Unhealthy Food

- It helps You Reduce the Amount of Alcohol You Drink
- It enables you to Avoid Using Drugs
- It Enables You to Exercise Your Body
- It allows you to Lose Weight
- It Helps You Quit Smoking
- It Enables You to Control Anger
- It Makes It Possible to Avoid Acting Impulsively and without Thinking
- Self-Discipline Helps You Overcome Unhealthy Habits

It Helps You Stop Eating Unhealthy Food

Overeat beef, eat junk food, and consume too much sugar is not suitable for your health. Because of the lack of discipline, a large number of people have no control over their food. We can't just change their eating habits because we lack the inner strength to do that.

If they had some control, the amount of food they eat could have been that junk food avoided and less sugar consumed. This would have strengthened their health and avoided health problems of all sorts.

Discipline would help you eat more healthily.

It Helps You Reduce the Amount of Alcohol You Drink

When you have control, reducing the amount of alcohol you're consuming is easier.

It could be okay for most people to drink a cup or two of alcohol. But when drinking turns into a habit that you don't have control over, it becomes a problem.

Possessing self-discipline will help you tolerate no constraints from drinking. Of course, before becoming a heavy drinker, one needs to develop that ability. Instead, the desire to drink too much would be harder to handle.

A heavy drinker can find it challenging to demonstrate restraint, and would, therefore, require additional means and assistance. Nevertheless, a large number of people who do not drink too much alcohol will consider possession of a certain degree of discipline to be most useful in keeping this habit in check.

It helps You Avoid Using Drugs

People who use drugs know they are not suitable for their health and can hurt it, but they cannot avoid using them because of a lack of discipline. If there was a way for them to strengthen their training, they could be made to reduce their use and even stop taking them. A person who doesn't use drugs and focuses on improving and strengthening their self-discipline has a better chance of abstaining from drugs and keeping away.

It Enables You to Exercise Your Body

Do you avoid physical activities? Do you prefer lounging on your couch, watching television and eating junk food when you get home from work? Will you keep saying that next week you're going to start going to the gym, but that never happens? When you establish even a small degree of self-discipline, you might make yourself go to the gym, go for a walk or regularly exercise your body with any kind of sport. Using your body is essential to your health. You don't resort to laziness and procrastination when you're getting discipline. It gives you the strength and resolves to decide to exercise your body and execute that decision as well.

It Helps You Lose Weight

How many people do you know who tried to lose weight? But were unable to keep up with their resolution? You may have tried to lose weight.

Too, but could not resist the delicious food, the tempting cakes, or the delightful ice cream. You may have tried some diets, but you left after one or two weeks. What stopped weight loss? It is missing adequate discipline and self-control. Just assume how slimmer you can also be if you have control over the amount of food you eat and can stay on with your nutrition until you lose the excess weight.

Some Discipline can help you lose weight.

It Helps You Quit Smoking

Smoking is an unhealthy habit, tried several times by most smokers to stop, but could not. They might say they manage this habit, and they can quit whenever they want, yet they don't, because they lack sufficient willpower and strength inside. Quitting smoking would be better if you are setting out to strengthen your discipline.

It Enables You to Control Anger

Anger is harmful to your health. It adversely affects the body and mind, increases blood pressure, and creates stress. You must prevent yourself from becoming angry, stop dragging into needless debates, and immediately raise your voice or exhibiting physical or verbal hostility. You need both discipline and inner strength to be able to do so.

It Makes It Possible to Avoid Acting Impulsively and without Thinking

Impulsivity implies a lack of control and unthinking behaviour. If you don't have the power of your acts and the words you're using, you could get into difficulty, and sometimes into risky situations. A small amount of discipline will reduce impulsiveness, bring common sense, and prevent you from getting tension and unreasonable risks.

Self-Discipline Helps You Overcome Unhealthy Habits

Smoking, overeating, eating junk and unhealthy food, laziness, procrastination, and other harmful habits do harm to your health. However, if you possess the ability to self-discipline, you can overcome these habits and build positive habits. To live a better and healthier life and have more control over your actions, you need some degree of self-discipline. Its possession allows you to withstand temptations and distractions, improve stamina, and help you overcome negative habits.

5.4 Self-Discipline at Workplace

Self-discipline is the ability to focus on a task or goal to achieve a given outcome. Like other attributes that could lead to your overall success, self-discipline is one that generates long-term sustained success. Self-disciplined people generally rely on a set of different characteristics, such as:

- Ambition
- Focus
- Organization
- Persistence
- Responsibility
- Resilience

- Strong work ethic

Self-discipline is the workplace that becomes a way to develop certain behaviours, thoughts, and habits that will help you complete tasks, reach objectives, and eventually achieve specific goals. Leaders are usually required to play down responsibilities. These responsibilities may include managing others, delegating work, engaging in problem-solving or conflict resolution, and working towards their tasks and objectives. Despite competing priorities, seeking an entire block of time can be challenging for a leader to concentrate its attention on any given task. The ability to resist desires, maintain concentration, and see jobs through to completion is self-discipline. It is characterized by the dedication and determination of a leader in devoting their attention to a mission until it has been satisfactorily completed. Leaders high on self-discipline aren't distracted easily. Given individual goals or criteria for their care, they may maintain focus. Work-based self-discipline helps members to pay full attention to the task at hand. Analysis has shown that leaders with a powerful sense of self-control and determination are more likely to engage in their work. Additionally, setting aside dedicated time to work on specific tasks displays two things directly reported. Second, it shows the kinds of activities or initiatives that their members prioritize. Second, it shows their members are willing and capable of rolling up their sleeves and sticking to their job. Not only is self-discipline a useful tool for leaders who are trying to do more work every day, but it can also inspire workers who follow their leader's example.

In assessing your level of self-discipline,

Ask yourself the following questions:

- Am I setting myself goals for what I want to accomplish each day?
- Do I take breaks throughout the day?

- Have I taken steps to limit the distractions and temptations that hinder my progress?
- Do I give myself a reasonable amount of time to complete tasks?
- Am I effectively delegating work and decision-making where possible?
- Am I mindful of my day-to-day work routine?

Improve Your Self-Discipline

REMEMBER THE RULES OF MOTIVATION

There are a few tips from the literature on motivation and setting goals that can help you improve your workplace persistence3. Next, place your targets where possible. These should be broad enough to create a sense of success in achieving the goal but small enough to be realistic and achievable. Bringing a big goal into smaller, more manageable pieces can help keep your motivation going over time. If you have a personally exciting and motivating purpose, you will find it easier to focus your attention on achieving this goal. Make sure to take the time to praise your efforts when you are completing a task, whether small or large. The process of setting realistic goals, working towards those goals, and celebrating your achievements will maintain your motivation and engagement in your tasks and help you stay motivated and concentrated for more extended periods.

TAKE FREQUENT BREAKS

Self-discipline is something of a muscle. Through practice, we will learn and strengthen our abilities. But we can also get tired and find our ability to remain exhausted in charge. The more in a day we use our self-control, the more depletes we consider this resource4.

Luckily, as with our muscles, taking a break from your job is a simple strategy for restoring the discipline and focus that was lost. Daily breaks should be arranged, taking time away from desks or computers. Furthermore, leaders will arrange breaks that are ideal for the research they address every day. For example, if you find that specific tasks leave you exhausted or tired, consider scheduling this task at a time when a long break or work requiring little active self-control will immediately follow it. Try to keep track of how you feel about your responsibilities. Doing so will allow you to manage your time more efficiently to get the most out of your day your self-control.

Remember, the types of activities a leader finds especially challenging or frustrating can differ among individuals. The work schedule and subsequent breaks should be tailored to your interests and needs.

Remove temptations and distractions:

Self-discipline is better improved with daily practice, as are many skills. It's a learned behaviour, not an innate ability we should teach ourselves to practice more often. One of the easiest ways to set yourself up for success is to take away from your job the things you find that bother you. That may look different across people. Shutting the door to your office may be enough for some to help keep their attention on hold. For others, silencing calls, shutting off cell phones, or blocking enticing websites are safer methods to stay focused? To start the distractions removal cycle, go about your day as you would usually do. Keep a note of what distracted you each time your attention is diverted from your job. Within a few days, you'll see patterns or distraction categories emerging, and identifying these lets, and you know how to avoid them. Remember, it will take time to change how you work, so be patient as you remove distractions from your working day. Competing priorities and urgently necessary tasks are often a fact of life for leaders, and diversions will sometimes be inevitable. Self-discipline helps you stay focused in the face of non-essential interruptions.

Start Doing These 3 Things Now to Increase Self-Discipline these steps can help you increase your self-control in the workplace:

Make a fresh start

Offer them a clean slate if you have an employee whose attention has been slipping, who is struggling to turn up on time, or keeps meeting deadlines. It is not so much the system of thought that can strengthen their determination but the marking of a new regime. When you've had your little talk with them, suggest things will change starting at 9 am on Monday, and they're more likely to see through their good intentions.

Make time to make decisions

Decision-making is one of those tasks which often fall solely upon leaders. It covers everything from deciding how to allocate resources, defining the unit's goals, and assigning each employee to work. Evidence has shown that decision-making is a tiring activity, and after making influential decisions5, leaders find it difficult to maintain self-control and concentration. Behave decision-making as any other task: give yourself adequate time to concentrate on making the right choice and recover from any stress that may result from this task. Forcing yourself to make essential decisions while juggling other goals will only ensure you feel overwhelmed and lead to low self-control.

Reduce the load:

While decision-making can often come down to leaders, delegation is a vital tool to avoid overloading yourself. Have your employee's input in decision making where possible, by either gathering more information that will help you make the right choices or by providing their advice and experience. This not only reduces the amount of work a leader takes, but the literature also indicates that involvement in some decision-making will boost employees' long-term self-discipline and motivation5. Delegating some of the work that goes into making decisions can be mutually beneficial to you and your employees.

Practice mindful meditation:

Meditation of mindfulness is gaining popularity within the work world and is often proposed as a solution to a variety of organizational problems. Proper mindfulness training, however, helps you enhance your concentration by learning to concentrate on a fixed point, such as your breath while allowing feelings or thoughts to flow through without influencing you. Regular meditation can have many positive effects on leaders. Still, in the case of self-discipline, the daily practice of mindfulness decreases impulsiveness, allowing you to maintain your concentration in control all day.

Visualize the results

A list of healthy intentions is one thing, but it has also been shown that fantasizing about success is bringing errant staff back on track. Encourage your workers to see the effect their performance will have on themselves and others, and it can make them leap out of the picture and envision something worth striving for.

Teamwork:

Any employee processes in a vacuum. Try to make self-discipline high on your hiring list of contributing factors, and those well-disciplined workers you take on should help pull the expectations of those who are more likely to disrupt. You can also inspire the employees to look out for each other and reassure each other when there are bad habits. No one has to report anything to the boss, but providing a sense of collective responsibility to your employees for the organization's performance can have a real effect. Check that they are in the right job. Instead of satisfying others, self-discipline is most possible when it's done for oneself. If you have a team member who, despite your efforts to support, is struggling to motivate themselves, they may just not be excited about their work. Have a friendly conversation with them to see what's going on, and talk about how else they might fit in with your company or how you could make their present position more acceptable.

Chapter 6 Mastering Self-Discipline

"Chains of habit are too light to be felt until they are too heavy to be broken." It is expectedly too easy for bad habits to ruin our health, finances, relationships, business and happiness. Only one bad habit can be the reason that destroys a dozen good ones.

Here's how to break the worst habits and set up for success.

6.1 Ways to Mastering Self-Discipline

People with a higher degree of self-control spend less time deciding whether to engage in activities that damage their wellbeing and can make more easily meaningful choices. They are not letting impulses or feelings dictate their choices. Instead, they make level-headed decisions. As a consequence, they tend to feel more content with their lives. There are exercises you can do to learn to discipline yourself and achieve the Will to lead a happier life. If you're looking to take control of your habits and decisions, here are some of the most powerful things you can do in order to master yourself.

Know your weaknesses.

We all have liabilities. Whether it's treated like potato chips or chocolate chip cookies, or apps like Facebook or the new addictive gaming device, they do have similar effects on us.

Recognize your shortcomings no matter what they may be. Too often, people either try to pretend they don't have their vulnerabilities or cover up any pitfalls in their lives. Face up to your failures. Until you do, you can't overcome anything.

Remove temptations.

As the saying goes, "out of vision, out of mind.

" It may sound dumb, but this sentence offers an influential recommendation. You'll significantly enhance your self-discipline by merely removing the greatest temptations from your life.

Do not buy junk food if you wish to eat healthier. Turn off notifications and silence your mobile phone if you want to boost your productivity at work. The fewer Distractions

Set clear goals and have an execution plan.

When you hope to achieve self-discipline, you'll need to have a clear vision of what you're trying to accomplish. You also need to get an idea of what you mean by performance. After all, it's easy to lose your way or get side-tracked, if you don't know where you are going.

A clear plan outlines every step you need to take to reach your targets. The figure who you are and what you're up to. Create a mantra to keep a focus on yourself. Successful individuals use this strategy to stay on track and set a clear finish line.

Build your self-discipline.

We're not born with self-discipline — it's a skill learned. And it requires daily practice and repetition, just like any other ability you wish to learn. Just like going to the gym, it takes a lot of work for the determination and self-discipline. It can be exhausting the effort and focus needed by self-discipline.

When time goes on, holding your Willpower in check will become more and more difficult. The challenge or decision, the more it can feel challenging to tackle certain activities that also require self-control. Thus work by daily diligence on building your self-discipline.

Create new habits by keeping it simple.

Initially, learning self-discipline and working to inculcate a new habit can feel overwhelming, mainly if you concentrate on the whole task at hand. Only keep it simple to avoid feeling threatened. Bridge your target into small, practical steps. Instead of trying to change everything at once, concentrate on regularly doing one thing and practice self-discipline with that objective in mind.

If you're trying to get into shape, start with 10 to 15 minutes of work out a day. If you are trying to achieve healthier sleeping habits, start every night by going to bed 15 minutes earlier. If you want to eat healthier, start with lunch the evening before you take it with you in the morning. Take steps for a boy. Finally, you can add more goals to your list when you're ready.

Eat often and healthy.

The feeling of hanging— the frustrated, depressed, irritated mood you get when you're hungry— is real and can have a significant impact on your Willpower. Evidence has shown that low sugar in the blood also weakens a person's determination and makes you grumpy and gloomy.

The ability to focus drops when you're hungry, and the brain doesn't function as well. In all ways, including food, exercise, work, and relationships, your self-control is likely to be reduced. And you fuel up with healthy snacks and regular meals to stay in control.

Change your perception of the force of Will.

The sum of a person's Willpower depends on their beliefs. When you know you have a small amount of Willpower, you are not likely to exceed those limits. If you don't put a limit on your self-control, you're less likely to kill yourself until you achieve your objectives.

In short, our internal willpower and self-control conceptions can decide how much of them we have. If you can overcome these implicit barriers and honestly believe you can, then you will be giving yourself an extra boost of motivation to make those ambitions a reality.

Give yourself a backup plan.

Psychologists use a method called "implementation goal" to improve motivation. That's when you offer yourself a plan to deal with a potentially challenging situation that you know you likely face. Imagine, for example, that you're focusing on healthier eating, but you're on your way to a party where food is being served.

Before you go, remind yourself that you will be sipping a glass of water instead of digging into a plate of cheese and crackers, and concentrate on mixing. Going in with a plan will help give you the mindset and the necessary self-control for the situation. You'll also save time by not having to make a sudden emotional decision.

Reward yourself.

Give yourself something to be enthusiastic about when you plan a reward to achieve your goals. Just like when you were a little child, getting something to look forward to gives you the drive to be productive.

Anticipation is high. This gives you something to reflect and concentrate on so that you don't just worry about what you're trying to change. And when you reach that goal, you will find a new target and a further incentive to keep moving forward.

Forgive yourself and move forward.

We still fall short, even with all of our best intentions and well-laid plans. It does happen. You're going to have ups and downs, big wins, and miserable defeats. The trick is to remain on the run.

If you are slipping, then remember what caused it and push on. Don't let yourself be wrapped up in remorse, rage or disappointment, for these feelings will only pull you further down and hamper future progress. Learn from your mistakes and forgive. Then get your head back into the game and focus on your goals.

6.2 Building Mental Toughness

Intelligence is helping you to be a successful person, but the commitment and mental toughness are mandatory. Keep track of those essential customs.

It's a well-known adage: In our happiness and success, what happens to us plays far less a role than our answers.

To develop and maintain the type of mental toughness that achievement requires, keeping your thoughts and self-talking positive and avoiding the habits that lead to negativity and unhealthy behaviours are crucial.

The most influential people are not those who show strength before us, but those who win fights we never see fighting against them.

Help keep yourself prepared by practicing good habits of mind and mentality for whatever comes your way tomorrow:

Emotional stability

Leadership also needs you, under pressure, to make the right decisions. You must keep your ability to stay objective and offer the same performance level no matter what you feel.

Perspective

When the world seems to have turned against you, mental strength lets you carry on. Learn how to keep your issues in a correct perspective without losing sight of what you need to achieve.

Readiness for change

If change is the only constant, then the most important features you can create are versatility and adaptability.

Detachment

If you can note that it's not about you, you can get through challenges and come out even more. Don't personally take anything or spend time asking Why me? Reflect instead on what you can control.

Strength under stress

Maintain resilience in the face of negative pressures by developing your capacity to deal with stressful situations.

Preparation for challenges

Life and company are packed with demands from everyday life, the occasional crisis, and unexpected twists. Make sure you have the means to deal with the professional and personal challenges you'll face sooner or later.

Focus

Hold the long-term consequences in mind to stay steady in the face of real or future obstacles.

The right attitude toward setbacks

Complications, unintended side effects, and total failures all form part of the landscape. Mitigate the damage, learn, and move on with the lessons that will benefit you in the future.

Self-validation

Don't worry about satisfying others: for anyone but the worst kind of waffler, that's a hit-or-miss proposition. Then, make a concentrated effort to do the right thing and to know what you mean

Patience

Don't expect results to come to fruition immediately, or rush things ahead of time. Anything worthwhile requires hard work and stamina; see everything as a work in progress.

Control

Avoid getting the power over to someone else. You are in control of your actions and emotions; your strength lies in controlling the way you react to what is happening to them.

Acceptance

Don't think about those things you don't have control over. Recognize that your reaction and attitude are the one thing you can always monitor and use these attributes effectively.

Endurance in the face of failure

Perspective failure as an opportunity to grow and keep improving, not just as a reason to give up. Be prepared to continue the effort until you get it right.

Unwavering positivity

Stay positive also — especially — when you come across negative people. Elevate them; never get down to yourself. Don't let naysayers spoil the spirit of what you achieve.

Contentment

Don't waste time envying the car, house, girlfriend, job, or family of anyone else. Instead, be thankful for what you've got. Rather than looking over your shoulder and becoming envious of what everyone else has, focus on what you've achieved and what you're going to make.

Tenacity

It comes down to just three words: Never give up.

A strong inner compass

When your sense of direction is deeply internalized, you never have to worry about becoming lost. Stay true to your course.

Uncompromising standards

Tough times or business problems aren't good reasons for lowering the bar. Stick to your expectations.

It takes practice and concentration to become a mentally healthy person. To fix them, it involves tuning in to your bad habits and making a point of learning new habits. And sometimes, it just means learning to get out of your way and letting things happen.

6.3 Improving Will Power for Better Self-Discipline

Willpower, Self-control and Self-discipline. These are many names that all mean the same thing: having the mental strength and attitude to do the things you know you must do consciously. Sure-even if you don't want to be emotional.

Through learning how to strengthen your strength, you'll learn how to enhance an ability that works in your life. It is associated with increased Willpower becoming happier, scoring higher on standardized tests, and earning more money. Willpower is also highly correlated with personal goals achievement.

But, what you may not know is that Willpower is a strength you can call upon–and, at the same time, it's also an ability you can develop.

Remove Temptation

Willpower is a resource that is limited-so don't waste it. You slowly deplete your Willpower every time you need to tell yourself "no" to temptation in front of you–and it takes time to replenish. So whenever possible: separate your life from the attractions.

For example, if you think you're watching too much TV and need to spend the next month on a project–cancel your cable, or physically unplug your TV from the wall. As a personal example, I know that if it's in the building, I'll eat junk food–so I'll never have any in my home.

Stabilize Blood Sugar

Low blood sugar is associated with diminished self-discipline. Avoid eating sugary foods such as candy or high sugar drinks. Of course, it's a bit of a catch 22 – it takes self-discipline to avoid eating tasty, sugary foods to begin with!

Sleep

Make sure you get enough of it. Research has shown that the ability to maintain focus on tasks suffers due to lack of sleep.

Enjoy Life

Positive psychological experiences refill your reservoir of self-discipline. So, all day long – take a few minutes to enjoy your life I love taking breaks and running, playing guitar, hiking, and doing other things that inspire me – find out what works for you.

Avoid and Reduce Stress

Tension has proven that self-discipline is depletive. Reducing commitments, breathing exercises, and yoga have helped me personally minimize anxiety in my life.

Research shows that having a mission and a target you're chasing will help mitigate the effects of reduced willpower as your willpower begins to get drained.

I'm taking you to step by step in The Action Solution through how to set a path for your life and a specific plan for achieving it. I use the same approach in my own life–and I am confident that it has resulted in sustaining a higher level of willpower and success in my life People with good intentions always fail –it's no guarantee that you'll succeed, but it certainly makes it more likely.

Self-Affirmations

Similar to positive emotional experiences, it has been shown that self-affirmations help to replenish diminished will power.

I like using my pages from the start. I designed them individually, so I could focus on one goal and one thought. Now my philosophy is to value your time.

Strengthen Your Willpower

Self-discipline is a strength–focus on small tasks you can manage, and slowly increase the ability to stick to more significant jobs.

Several workout examples include straightening your body and using the non-dominant hand to perform tasks. Start brushing your teeth, for instance, with the non-dominant hand. Try to switch the hand that holds the dishes in and the side that cleans the dishes in.

6.4 The Strength and Stamina of Willpower

Self-control or strength of will refers to your ability to resist temptation by being overly negative or positive about yourself to complete a self-report measure of this aspect of willpower fast. Consider each object, instead, and compare yourself with similarly aged peers. Unlike strength or volunteer intensity, willpower is analogous to stamina.

Self-monitoring

At this moment in time, the ratings are arbitrary tests of the strength and endurance of your Will. Because they are subjective, they are state-dependent-when you feel puny; you are likely to score more poorly on these tests than when you feel confident. What's more, what's being measured, your Will's strength and endurance change over time. Unlike physical strength and endurance, exercise increases willpower, and disuse atrophies. I, therefore, recommend that you periodically retake these tests and use the results to guide your training.

Success & Failure

This is terrible for failure. Deficiency leads to failure. Performance diminishes self-efficacy more than wasting time, setting a bad precedent, and creating negative emotional states. All strength and resilience are linked to your self-efficacy. People who think they can't succeed don't work with enough dedication and tend to give up their efforts as soon as it gets complicated.

Consequently, the outcome of their actions appears to affirm their original conviction. On the other hand, this self-confirming bias works positively for those who respect the heroic nature of their challenge and their strength and endurance. There is substantial empirical support for the idea that: "Nothing succeeds like success." Be mindful that for most people, negative beliefs about one's strength and endurance are more common and reasonable, and so measuring Will's power appears to result in an overly negative evaluation. Much of this course's section on Emotion-Focused Coping is designed to free you from this negative bias. Be cautious about too critical assessments about yourself before you revisit the article. I'm not saying you're positively biased, but avoiding negative biases is significant. A muscle may be weak due to lack of exercise and preparation, or nervous due to lack of fatigue. Likewise, your willpower may be compromised by excessive short-term use or insufficient long-term exercise of the mental faculties associated with will exercise. The treatment depends on the cause of the infirmity:

Failure makes this horrible. Deficiency triggers failure. Failure more than a waste of time diminishes self-efficacy, sets a bad precedent, and produces negative emotional states. Your power and endurance are tied to your effectiveness. People who think they can't be successful don't have enough commitment to work and generally give up their efforts as soon as it gets tough. If Will's deficiency is due to insufficient growth, the cure consists in the exercise of the mental faculties involved.

Wherever possible, they are making subjects practice improving posture, keeping track of food, speaking in full sentences, or preventing contractions that resulted in enhancing self-regulatory capabilities. A wide array of mental exercises are listed in this course's Emotion-Focused Coping section. High-risk situations arise when environmental factors–such as social pressure, negative emotional states, etc.– facilitate recurrence. Will exercise means over-riding specific forces and doing as you wish. That is an impressive feat, and as far as we learn, it can only be achieved by humans. Exercising Will is similar to walking up a hill with a stone. The force that has to come from within to manipulate behavioural and emotional responses. The tools needed to generate power are precious. You are bound to follow the path of least resistance when they are insufficient to circumvent the causal-and-effect rules–such as the PIG or the Rule of Procedure. Therefore, an essential part of Will's exercise is the creation and maintenance of the cognitive and motivational resources needed to deal with the high-risk circumstances you are expected to experience .Lead a healthy, purposeful life in which you take good care of your body.

Rest and sleep

From any other sleep advantage, it's essential to allow the creature you inhabit time to recover the biological energy needed to exercise Will.

Simply being asleep doesn't seem as critical as giving the brain time away from the crisis to allow time for the tired faculties to recover.

Research shows that glucose management completely reversed the brain changes caused by depletion. This is trying to find to be particularly interesting because it suggests that ego depletion in some parts of the brain causes the activity to rise and decline in others. When glucose is low, the brain doesn't stop working. It starts doing some things and continues to do others. Impulsivity increases because its inhibitory influence is less exercised by the intelligent processing system, which requires energy to do its labor. Instead of following the path of the most significant advantage (taking into account the long-term consequences of its choices), the behavior of the creature is determined by the immediate local payoffs.

Do what you can to avoid physical exhaustion and invest in ego-filling activities–e.g., holidays, flowing activities, regular exercise. Getting to do these things requires the very cognitive resources that we are doing to enhance those things. As with many self-referential paradoxes, both contradictory findings are valid. In some ways, investing your willpower strengthens rather than depletes it, especially when taking into account the long-term outcomes. Develop your Coping Skills Focused on Emotion. Heightened emotional states not only produce state-dependent distortions of behaviours in appraisals, perceptions, and reactions, but they also drain the cognitive resources needed to exercise Will. Prayer of serenity is an excellent guide to enhancing Will. In specific, too:

Be detached from reactions to things you do not control, so that you do not fritter away your precious cognitive resources in meaningless attachments.

Of particular concern is the unnecessary emotionality caused by neurotic, ruminative self-focus, or pointless attachments to things you don't control, like the past, what other people do, natural disasters, etc. Put on proper preparation and results. You deserve to be gratified with your perseverance because it is your duty. Motivation to do the hard things to do can be strengthened by a commitment to do what it takes to be noble-just don't let it get out of control.

6.5 Self-Discipline Is a Key to Success

Self-discipline is the most important attribute to becoming successful. It helps you stay focused on achieving your goals, gives you the gumption to keep up with challenging tasks, and enables you to overcome obstacles and discomfort as you push yourself to new heights.

What is Self-Discipline exactly? It is the ability to control your impulses, emotions, reactions, and behaviours; it allows you to forego short-term satisfaction and gain in favour of long-term happiness. When you want to answer "yes," it's saying "no." It's not about living a restrictive, boring life that is empty of pleasure. In reality, being self-disciplined in all areas of your life is next to impossible. Instead of trying to get involved in everything you do, use it to concentrate on what's most important.

Want more discipline? Check out some of the tips:

- You can't achieve your goals without discipline, so add a self-discipline list to your target list; it will keep you focused on the behaviours and tasks you need to accomplish what you want. For instance, one of my goals is to make our customers more noticeable. My discipline list includes things like "call three customers a week" and "send five thank you cards a month."

- Keep track of what you need and get done to achieve your goals, using a daily "to do" list. Consider using online tools to coordinate to prioritize the routine checklists.

- When you've completed a task, it feels good to check the little boxes; it can even motivate you to finish one more thing on your list at the end of the day just to feel the satisfaction of checking out another. Make sure that your list of "to-do" matches your list of disciplines, so you stay on track.

- Find out what are your barriers to success. For example, I'm easily distracted by texts, meetings, and people walking into my office; to reach my goal of having more customer contact, I shut my office door as soon as I get to work and make calls, send thank you notes and answer customer emails. Then I check my "do" list out and move on with my day. Looking to lose weight? Get your junk food out of the house. Do you want to be more productive on the job? Close your application by email and only check your emails twice a day. Do you want to get into shape? Wake up early and work out so that you don't lose focus at the end of the day when you are tired. Minimize or eliminate all temptations and obstacles to attaining the most critical objectives.

- Tell others about your goals. Sticking to something is easier when you've made a public commitment; thinking about failing in front of others can be a motivation to stick to it. These individuals can also help hold you accountable.

- I know the saying goes, "Don't do it for others; do it for yourself," but when I consider how my actions, behaviours, emotions, and impulses affect others, I found that I am much more disciplined. Contrary to common belief, using outside outlets to boost motivation is OK. Even external motivators are sometimes more effective than internal ones. Find the goal beyond yourself to create a higher chance of success.

- Through forming patterns, you create discipline. When something becomes a habit, you do not need any more willpower to push you to do it. One of my goals was to do more yoga, for example. I committed for 30 days to do it 30 minutes a day. I've seen those advantages that I've stuck with. Now I'm getting up an hour earlier in the morning to start my day off with an hour of yoga... without setting the alarm.

- Stop making excuses. Don't wait until tomorrow; just do it now. Falls off the railcar? Start right away. It's too hard to stop telling yourself something or that you can't change. Don't blame the circumstances on others. Excuse-making is a self-disciplining killer. Can accomplish more by adopting an attitude of "I can do this."

- You are the master of fate, the creator of life. If you want a specific look and feel for your life, then you have to cultivate the discipline to get there. While it seems counterintuitive, the more self-disciplined you are, you'll find yourself happier and healthier.

Reasons Why Self Discipline Is Important For Success

Self-discipline is the secret to lifelong success. Without it, you can't succeed in life. Successful people will always advise you to stay disciplined. But the question is, "why is self-discipline essential to lifetime success?"

Self-discipline helps you become an irresistible driving force in your life to achieve the highest level.

The first thing you need to do is restrain yourself if you want to become productive in life.

Let's find out why self-discipline is essential for success.

Self-discipline creates a habit.

Habits can make you or break you. In your life, self-discipline produces a pattern that only builds up through discipline.

Most of the people in their lives never remain disciplined because they are lazy. Yet laziness is also a form of habit.

Successful individuals are motivated to work and remain consistent with it. And it becomes something of a habit. This is what attracts lifetime success.

It helps you get things done.

It is essential to have the self-discipline to get things done. Whether you commit to reading books or complete a task in a timeline, it can be anything.

By disciplining yourself to complete every single thing, you build a personality around it.

This habit makes you a lifetime accomplisher.

For performance, self-discipline is critical. Because it helps you stay happy in life, and you will do anything you want in life when you're consistent.

It helps you to focus on it.

We live in a society that lined with distractions. Self-discipline lets you concentrate on the goals you set. It helps you to stick to the work that you want to do to make it succeed.

If you concentrate on your target, you'll achieve every single thing you need to accomplish.

Successful people get a sharp focus on the laser.

They always look forward to their lifelong goals and achievements.

This helps them attain a high success level in their lives.

It boosts your self-esteem and work ethic.

Success comes to those who believe in themselves, and are the room's most hardened worker. Self-discipline allows you to, at the same time, increase your self-esteem and work ethic.

By sticking to it, you improve your work ethic when you restrain yourself.

It'll help you achieve your goals.

Nonetheless, you'll start to improve your self-esteem and faith in your work when you achieve your goals every day.

For success, this is the reason why self-discipline is necessary.

It helps you to achieve mastery.

Success comes down to those who are not beginner's masters; you have to be master at something if you want success.

Through putting up the work and spending up to 10,000 hours on one thing, you become master.

Through training comes Leadership. Many people fail because they know nothing about mastering, whereas there's one thing successful people do and practice.

So, this is how self-discipline yields dominance and mastery.

It helps you to become the best version of yourself.

Success only comes when it is warranted. With the attitude you already have, you can't succeed. Therefore, every single day, you need changes.

To become successful in life, you need to become the best version of yourself.

Self-discipline helps you improve your daily routine. You feel better and better every day when you do it regularly.

So, that is why self-discipline is vital to life's success and development.

Self-discipline is the cornerstone of success. You have to have discipline if you want to be successful in life. Otherwise, the people who are disciplined would knock you out.

You have unlimited potential in your life to reach the highest level. All that's required is self-discipline.

6.6 Secrets of Self-Discipline

Self-discipline. Let's face it frankly. It's a work in progress for most of us, wrapped in good intentions, timidity, and feelings of failure. But that hasn't got to be. Self-discipline is a skill, as is everything else. Maybe every day will be flawless, but every day is progress— with its mistakes and small victories— and that's what self-discipline is all about.

I have rounded up steps that you can take to build self-discipline today. This essay, combined with a good understanding of what self-discipline is, and a little motivation, give you the resources you need to develop a self-disciplinary practice in everything you do.

Developing self-discipline does more than helping you move your career forward. Assisting humans to has been proven:

- Achieving long-term goals-Self-discipline allows people to resist immediate impulses in favour of higher-impact, long-term objectives. In her 2016 work on perseverance and the "passion for long-term goals," also known as grit, Grit expert Angela Duckworth contributes to this. Her study found "the achievement of challenging goals involves not only talent but also a sustained and focused application of talent over time," or what we would call self-discipline.

- Reduce anxiety-We each have our vices when we're overwhelmed (Hi, my name is Meg, and I procrastinate when stressed). If we feel negative emotions, humans tend to get distracted by doing something else or worrying about it. Indeed, a 2016 study found improving self-control during school testing may help students deal with anxiety-related issues.

- Increase physical health-This is probably quite obvious, but people who demonstrate natural self-discipline are better able to resist the use of substances such as tobacco and alcohol that are harmful to their health. Self-control is also linked to lower obesity and addiction levels.

- Relationships affect positively-Yep; self-discipline can also make the connections stronger. Psychology today says, "The ability to self-control is an ability to take empathetic perspective— the ability to step outside one's point of view." By taking these steps, we can override our automatic defensive reactions and adopt more constructive behaviours that contribute to healthier, happier relationships.

- Become more robust-Easily bouncing back from adversity? Self-discipline will show resilience. The more resilient you are, the more you have power over urges and delayed gratification. Psychology Today states, "A positive person has confidence in their own ability to effectively handle the difficulties and circumstances of life."

- Feel happier-The more successful you are, the happier and more innovative you are. The more we feel in control of the root of our behaviour, the better sense we have of wellbeing— and this makes us happy!

Know where you struggle

Start by writing down what you've been doing in a day. Then think about what you value and ask yourself if your behaviours uphold those values. There are probably a few things that you do every day that don't honour those values (hey, we're only human — we all have a few).

Know how you succeed

Meet your friends and inquire about their evenings. A coffee getaway to the kitchen. Lunch with the team. Local coffee shop an afternoon walk. All these short trips add up to a considerable amount of time away from work. Building relationships with co-workers is important and giving yourself mental and physical breaks throughout the day.

But it is also essential, to be honest about the trends in your work. It's not good if non-work-related events consume your mornings, and that's when you're most productive. Know when you're doing your best work, and schedule it around.

Visualize your outcome

The brain does not discriminate between memories that are real and imagined. And, if you visualize anything vividly, the brain chemistry will change as if you had witnessed it.

Visualizing positive results such as, "If I make it to the top of our activity board, I'll treat myself to an outstanding meal," gives you the positive feelings associated with rising to the leader board while minimizing feelings of insecurity. This makes it easier for you to conquer anxious symptoms and take actionable steps to achieve your goals.

Don't wait for it to feel right

If you are waiting for the perfect schedule, your office to be clutter-free, or your inbox to hit a manageable level, you may never get started on the work that needs to be done. Each moment, accept yourself as getting just what you need to do your best job — because, well, it does.

Start small

Some ideas from this list? Ready to ruin your bad habits and turn into the perfect salesperson or employee? Small start. Refurbishing your work habits within a week is a burnout and catastrophe recipe.

Alternatively, pick a few tiny behaviours to concentrate on each week. You may decide to bring your coffee to the office for week one to avoid the morning rabbit hole known as "the break room" in favour of getting the right to work.

With a week of progress under your belt, you may be blocking a few hours through Friday afternoon on your calendar to complete administrative tasks such as adding prospect notes to the CRM or responding to unanswered emails. After a couple of weeks of changing one habit at a time— you may be shocked how much more successful and self-disciplined you have become.

Get a mentor

There are things that you can speak to a mentor about that you might not feel comfortable sharing with a friend or boss. If I want to stop wasting so much time when I'm supposed to be prospecting on social media, I would feel better to bring the challenge to my mentor rather than my boss.

Generally speaking, mentors have more experience, know you well, and can give you the advice and feedback you need to succeed— not just in your current job, but in your future.

Practice, fail, and start over

It's not that self-disciplined people never have days to eat all the doughnuts in the kitchen, waste 45 minutes on social media, and lose two opportunities before 10 a.m. It is they do these things, then the next morning they wake up and try to make better decisions.

The act of trying, failing, and trying again is self-discipline.

Know how you'll measure progress

If you do not see how you're going to track improvement, it's going to be hard to see if you're will. If your goal is to book more meetings in the first half of the month, begin by determining how many sessions you would like to book. So work backward to figure out how many sessions each week you will want and how long each will take to finalize.

Once you've determined your goal details, decide what it looks like to be a success. Are you shooting just for the total number? Will it count if a last-minute meeting cancels? Should the meeting cause a demo? Determine what the performance is so that you can calculate it.

Take care of yourself

If you are killing yourself to achieve this, self-discipline is worth very little. Everybody works the odd 28-hour day (those are there, right?), but if you burn the midnight oil for weeks or months to end up being more "self-disciplined," you've missed the point.

Part of the self-discipline is to look after yourself. All-day breaks, a healthy diet, plenty of sleep, and healthy relationships make the world — and we — go round. In reality, studies show mindfulness activities such as taking a short walk, observing five things around you, or recognizing two smells can increase workplace productivity.

Treat yourself

Want to stick to your good manners? Studies prove the key to rewarding yourself. Deprivation means we tend to justify bad behaviours. Often this sounds like, "I won this," or "I deserve it," — and it's often the beginning of the end of our development.

Give yourself sweets, instead, in the practice of self-discipline. Such therapies — whether you're enjoying a nice dinner or a new pair of shoes — can help you feel energized, healed, and never taken away.

Forgive Yourself

As importantly, when you slip, you have to forgive yourself. We've been thinking about it in point eight, but you're going to fail — it's unavoidable. What matters is that you keep moving on. You have to forgive yourself for doing that. Just my fantastic manager, told me, "It's not about giving yourself grace not to measure up. When you wake up late, hurry to the office, and forget to bring the coffee that thrusts you into the break room rabbit hole for 30 minutes of co-worker talk and three prospect calls short of your daily goal, take a rational look at the situation.

Have you failed to achieve your aim? Hey. Are you going to have to make some more calls tomorrow? Apparently. Will that have any bearing on your success in the long term? Nothing. Once you have looked at your slip's impact, you can decide how to move forward and get back on track. Before going to bed, ensure your alarm is set.

7. Conclusion

Achieving self-discipline may be difficult, but to lead a healthy personal and professional life, it is essential. A self-disciplined person makes optimum use of the time. Hence, he can achieve more and do more work as compared to a person who is not self-disciplined. We need to take into account that our students and children need to have organization and consistency in their lives. Discipline gives flexibility to our students and children. This gives them structure for not only the classroom but for their everyday lives and their futures. Children can't learn this information without it being taught to them, and some teachers and educators do not realize the importance of it. If our students and children did not have this structure, there is a lot at stake. Their grades could struggle, their social lives could flounder, and many other wrongs could go on in the lives of these children.

Discipline is necessary for all achievements, especially great achievements. Without training there can be no scientific advances (egg, no penicillin), no entrepreneurial, industrial or technological progress (egg, no mass-produced motor car), no settled system of law and order, no literary achievement and no exploration and development of a new land because all of these matters require the trained and balanced minds and bodies. We should, therefore, make some efforts to achieve self-discipline. The benefits of willpower are stark in the realm of prosperity and personal development. Even though the role of willpower is vital, you should not utilize it as your primary strategy.

Studies about people with the most willpower are thought-provoking.

When you learn how to improve your willpower, you learn how to strengthen a skill that helps across your life.

Improved willpower is associated with being happier, scoring higher on standardized tests, and earning more money. Willpower is also highly correlated with accomplishing personal goals.

People with the most self-discipline spend less time resisting temptations than others. You will need to cultivate your willpower muscle (enlarging the tank), which in turn gives you tremendous possibilities and will to act.

You will then use this "will" to make habits, and then those habits will make self-discipline in your life for you. Take the first step to change, and your life will start to change. Self-discipline also helps to increase our self-confidence. Self-discipline implies using rational thinking to control our actions and not emotions. This is the essence of proactive conduct. The more self-disciplined a person is, the more effective he is likely to be in his personal life & interpersonal relations. Dynamic nature can be developed with consistent effort to change our habits, which results in better self-discipline.

The better we're able to stay self-disciplined, the more confidence we'll develop because we'll know we can trust ourselves to stick to what needs to be done to achieve what we want.

8. References:

Prater, M. (2020). *Secrets of Self-Discipline: How to Become Supremely Focused*. [Online] Blog.hubspot.com. Available at: **https://blog.hubspot.com/sales/self-discipline**.

Very well Family. (2020). *Self-Discipline and Your Tween' School Success*. [Online] Available at: **https://www.verywellfamily.com/self-discipline-and-school-success-3288069**.

Forbes.com. (2020). *5 Proven Methods for Gaining Self Discipline*. [Online] Available at: **https://www.forbes.com/sites/jennifercohen/2014/06/18/5-proven-methods-for-gaining-self-discipline/#3a1addb43c9f**.

Sassoon, R. (2020). *Self-Discipline Benefits and Importance*. [Online] Successconsciousness.com. Available at: **https://www.successconsciousness.com/self_discipline.htm**.

Indeed.com. (2020). *Self-Discipline: Definition and Examples | Indeed.com*. [Online] Available at: **https://www.indeed.com/career-advice/career-development/self-discipline**.

Patterson, R. (2020). *8 Techniques for Building Unshakable Self-Discipline*. [Online] College Info Geek. Available at: **https://collegeinfogeek.com/self-discipline/**.

Littlethingsmatter.com. (2020). *Becoming a Disciplined Person*. [Online] Available at: **http://www.littlethingsmatter.com/blog/2011/02/01/becoming-a-disciplined-person/**.

Mistermagica.blogspot.com. (2020). *10 Characteristics of Self-Disciplined Achievers*. [Online] Available at: **http://mistermagica.blogspot.com/2007/05/10-characteristics-of-self-disciplined.html**.

Inc.com. (2020). *18 Powerful Ways to Build Your Mental Toughness*. [Online] Available at: **https://www.inc.com/lolly-daskal/18-powerful-ways-to-build-your-mental-strength.html**.

Medium. (2020). *The Secret of Raising a Self-Disciplined Child*. [Online] Available at: https://medium.com/@babycouture/the-secret-of-raising-a-self-disciplined-child-30b647a18f82.

CPSIA information can be obtained
at www.ICGtesting.com
Printed in the USA
LVHW021707011220
672997LV00006B/730